Tool Box Hapkido

ISBN 978-0-615-44057-6

Introduction

Hapkido literally means the art of coordinated power. It is a Korean art that is a form of unarmed self-defense based on circular techniques. The art includes joint locks, sweeps, throws, kicks and punches. It is a complete art that focuses on three basic skills:

- Non-resistance. Meeting your opponent with minimum force to deflect the attack and not clash with the power of the attack.
- Circular motion. Which is used to both counter the opponent's attack and return the attack in kind.
- The Water Principle. This principle allows the Hapkido practitioner to flow in and through your opponent.

This is not a complete treatise on Hapkido. Hapkido is a large art with a variety of strikes, kicks, throws and locks. These particular portions of the art are considered hard side training because they emphasize force and power. In short, they have a hard impact to your opponent. There are also throws and locks that lean toward the soft side of the art. These techniques have more of a flow and require little power. They are still very effective, but their initial impact to your opponent is soft. There are also other elements of soft side training, with emphasis on breathing techniques and Ki training. There are many good texts on the whole art already out there. This text is not trying to be an overall source for Hapkido knowledge, but to provide a basic toolkit. The refining of these tools will take time on the mat working and experimenting. I did say experimenting. You need to take the basic concept shown and play with it a little. See how it works (or doesn't work) in other applications. You will begin to learn how small variations in your opponent's position or your own can totally change the technique. Differences in size and weight will also matter. You will be able to work certain techniques better on a larger opponent than a smaller one and vice versa. In short you need to become comfortable with the technique and begin to make it your own.

I was motivated to produce this collection for two main reasons. The first was Hapkido captured my interest and has held it through 10 years of training. I am analytical by nature and I tend to want to break things down into small pieces and look at each piece intently. I also enjoy putting things together to accomplish an end goal. This is also how the title of the book you hold in your hand came about, Toolbox Hapkido. I consider each self defense technique a tool that is available in your self defense toolbox. As we add techniques, we add tools. This gives you more options.

This text was borne from hours and hours on the mat performing technique after technique and having them performed on me. I wanted to take some of the core techniques that I have learned in my training and highlight my preferred go to moves. The application section will provide viable techniques that can be used in real situations to some success. The ones shown here are also broken down into three levels: Basic, Intermediate and Advanced. Each section is arranged for a variety of situations and positions to show a diverse number of possible applications. It goes without saying that the techniques shown here are by no means comprehensive. Think of them as one possible option for getting out of a situation.

I will introduce some core Hapkido techniques and the mechanics behind them. The techniques will be broken down step by step with pictures to aid in the understanding. The joint manipulations will be broken down by target joint with examples shown of joint manipulations utilized in the application section.

The method of flowing from one technique to another or chaining will also be covered. Ideas will be given on which techniques tend to chain best together and some examples will be given on chaining sequences.

Finally, please play with the techniques. Use them in situations not spelled out here (in a controlled environment, please) and see how they work. What works differently. What doesn't work due to key pieces being missing in that application and more. In short, have fun with it.

This text could not have to come together without the outstanding instructors I have had over the years and the number of partners that worked (and continue to work) with me during my training. I would like to give special thanks to:

Jim Cokonis: for introducing me to this art for the first time.

Debra Disney: for being the primary instructor in my training. Ms. Disney is also one of the primary subjects of the photos used in this book to show the techniques.

Matt Thompson: for getting me to look at things from a different perspective when I get too focused on one specific direction.

Master Hee Wk Kim: for allowing me to continue my Hapkido training when I thought my time had passed and who continues to challenge and enhance my knowledge

Finally I would like to thank my family, for without them I would not have had the time to put into this that I do. Also thanks to Devin and Jesse for their time in being Ms. Disney's opponent in the pictures. Thanks also to Jessey for being part of the cover image.

Ahead of you is a view on the art of Hapkido that will give you a taste of what it can offer and challenge you to experiment and learn.

Core Techniques

Core Techniques

Live Hand

You will see in this text the term Live Hand used frequently. All this really means is opening the hand from a closed fist situation to one with fingers wide and outstretched. This shrinks the circumference of your wrist to allow you to create space to escape in a grabbing situation. You can use this space to escape the grab via the opponent's thumb, which is the weakest part of the grip, and apply the desired technique. The escape itself takes little or no strength, just moving the trapped arm out via the opponent's thumb in a sliding motion with your thumb pointing toward your chest and rotating toward it.

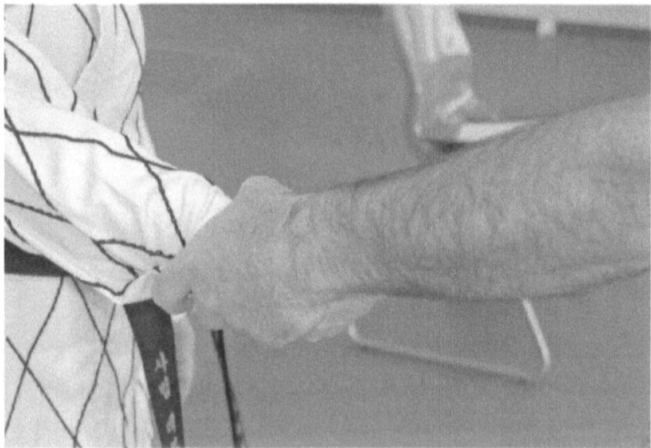

Figure 1: Live Hand, hand in fist

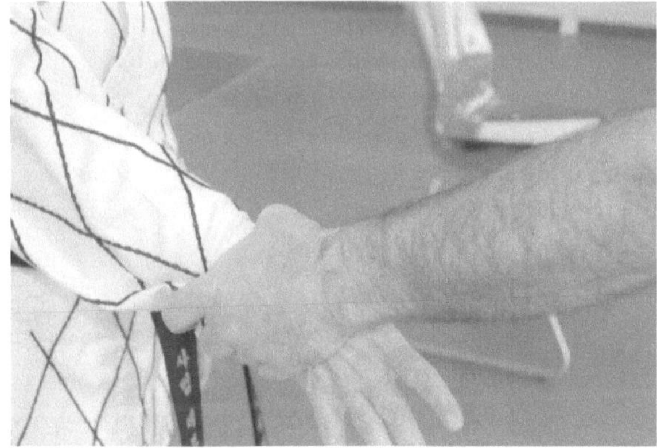

Figure 2: Live Hand, hand open

Joint Manipulation

This text will concentrate on joint manipulations as seen in Hapkido. A joint manipulation will move the target joint in a direction it was not made to move or a direction that causes the opponent pain. It is basic human anatomy, our joints were made to only move in certain directions. Moving them in direction other than that will cause pain, dislocation and breakage.

We will cover three main joint targets for these manipulations:

1. The Wrist
2. The Shoulder
3. The Elbow (in an arm bar situation)

The Wrist

The wrist manipulation manipulates the joint in a non-natural motion to cause pain with possible dislocation or destruction of the joint if taken to a full force situation. The wrist will move forward to back to a point depending on flexibility and side to side with no issues. The wrist manipulation moves the wrist either past the point of comfort in a forward/back or side to side motion, or rotates the wrist along a path that causes pain and discomfort. The rotation is normally done by utilizing the opponent's thumb joint as a handle of sorts with your hand gripping the thumb socket and rotating the wrist to either the outside or inside to cause pain.

The illustrations show examples of wrist rotation in an upward and side to side situation. Note in the upward rotation in Figure 3 the opponent's pinky fingers are on top and rotated upward toward the ceiling. In Figure 4 a side to side rotation of the wrist is shown utilizing your wrist to push the wrist up while the other hand pulls the opponent's hand down.

Figures 5 and 6 show the basics of an outside and inside rotation. When we say inside, we mean inward toward the body. An outside rotation is away from the body.

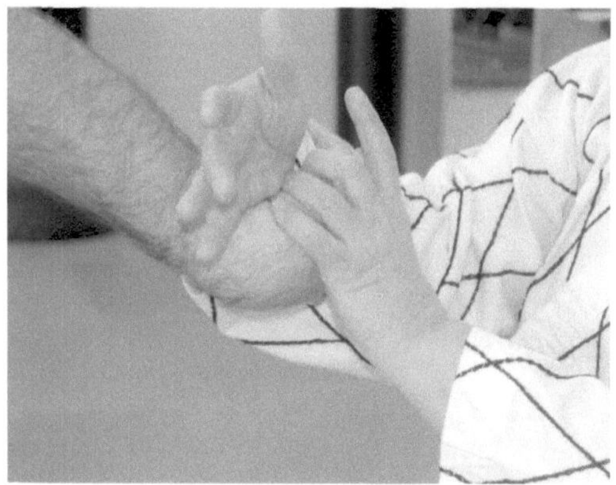

Figure 3: Rotation of wrist upward

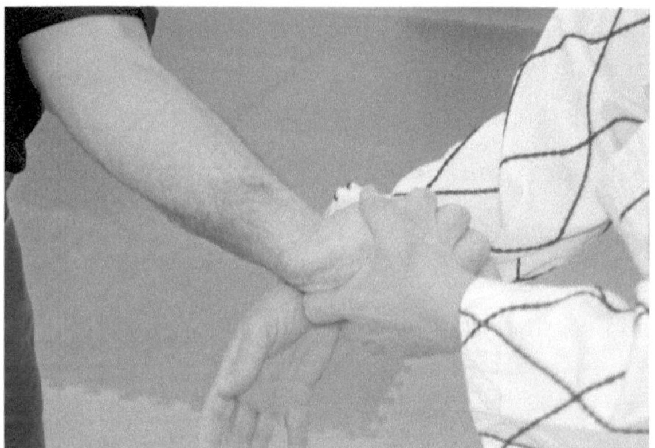

Figure 4: Side rotation of wrist

Figure 5: Inside wrist manipulation

Figure 6: Outside wrist manipulation

There are seven total wrist manipulations that we will show in this text. They are as follows:

Two Hands Outside Wrist Manipulation – Figure 7

- Place both thumbs to the rear of the opponent's hand with the fingers gripping the palm of the opponent's hand.
- Apply pressure with an outward rotation of the opponent's wrist away from the body.

Figure 7: Two hands outside wrist manipulation

Single Hand Outside Wrist Manipulation – Figure 8

- Place thumb between the knuckles of the back of the hand with fingers wrapping around the thumb to the palm.
- Fingers grasp around the thumb. Utilize thumb as a handle for the technique.
- Rotation will be toward the opponent's wrist and outward, away from the body.
- Assist with the off hand if needed. To assist place hand in a knife hand across the knuckles of the opponent's hand.

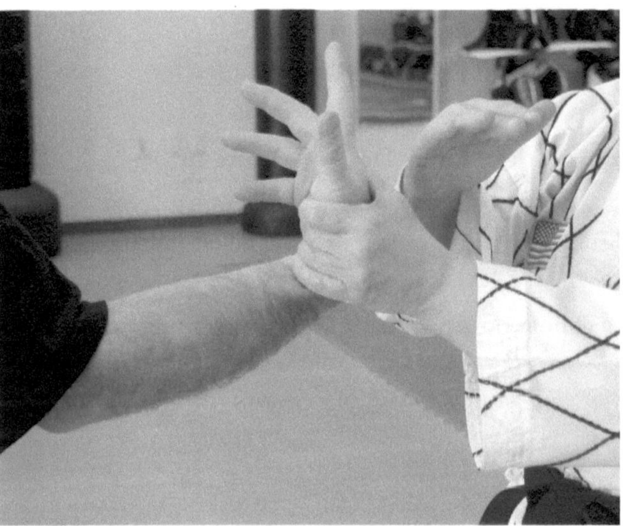

Figure 8: Single hand outside wrist manipulation

Bone to Bone Wrist Manipulation Pinky Up – Figure 9

- Rotate over the wrist with arm and place pressure downward with the wrist bone to the opponent's wrist bone to lock wrist in place.
- Grab the opponent's hand with the other hand across the back of the hand with fingers to the backside of the hand and the thumb toward the opponent's thumb. Lift the opponent's hand up slightly. The opponent's hand will be pinky side up.

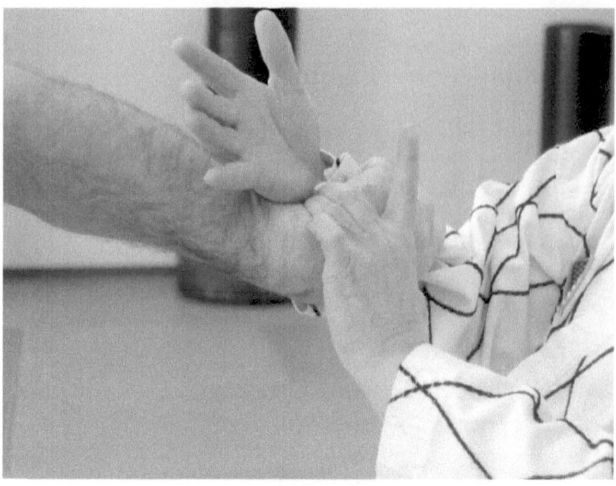

Figure 9: Bone to bone wrist manipulation pinky up

Bone to Bone Wrist Manipulation Pinky Down – Figure 10

- Rotate under the wrist with your wrist keeping the wrists tight, pressure is generated by lifting upward. Your thumb will be on top and pointing upward.
- The other hand will hold the opponent's hand tightly to the rotating hand so bone to bone contact can be initiated.

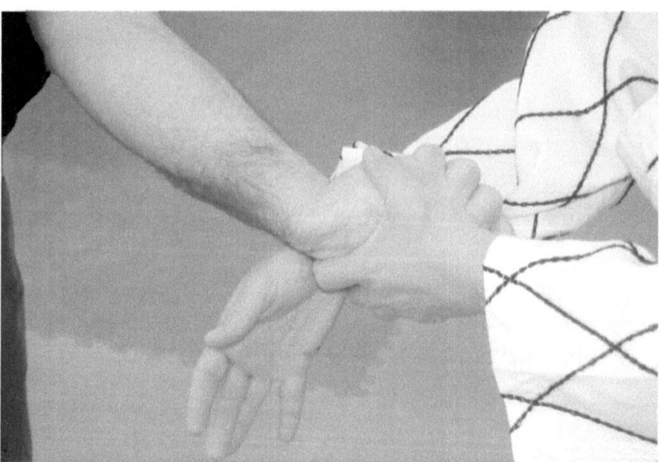

Figure 10: Bone to bone wrist manipulation pinky down

Z-Lock – Figure 11

- Opponent's hand is pinky side up.
- Rotate the held hand upward and away from the opponent's body.
- Other hand will hook into the opponent's elbow crook of the held arm with the pointer finger to control the arm. Collapse the opponent's elbow toward them causing their arm to take of a Z shape.
- Pull the held hand upward and push the elbow downward to apply pressure.

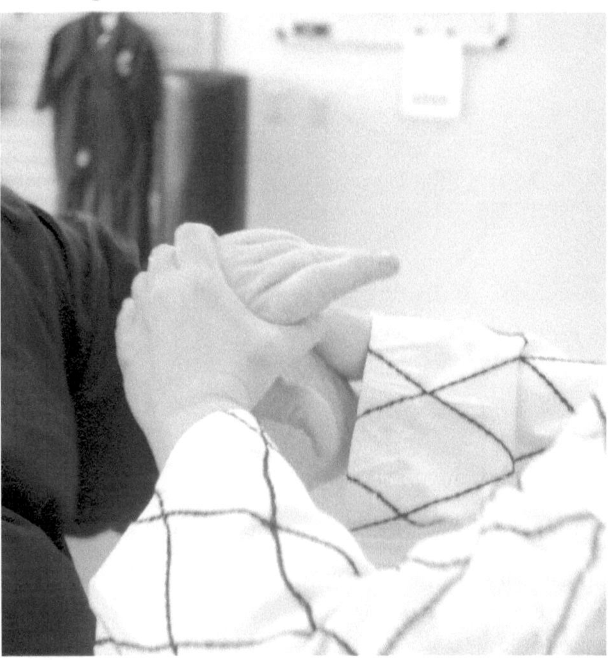

Figure 11: Z-lock

Pump-Handle Lock – Figure 12

- Opponent's hand will be pinky side up and thumb down.
- Grasp hand around the palm of the opponent to control the hand, thumb will be on the bottom of the hand.
- The other hand will grab the opponent's forearm toward the wrist.
- Pull the forearm down while bringing the hand up to apply pressure.

Figure 12: Pump-handle lock

Clamshell Lock – Figure 13

- Hold the opponent's hand with your palm facing theirs.
- Place the other hand over the back of the opponent's hand
- Rotate the hand on the back of the opponent's hand downward while bringing the other hand upward to apply pressure. This rotation will cause the pain we are looking for.

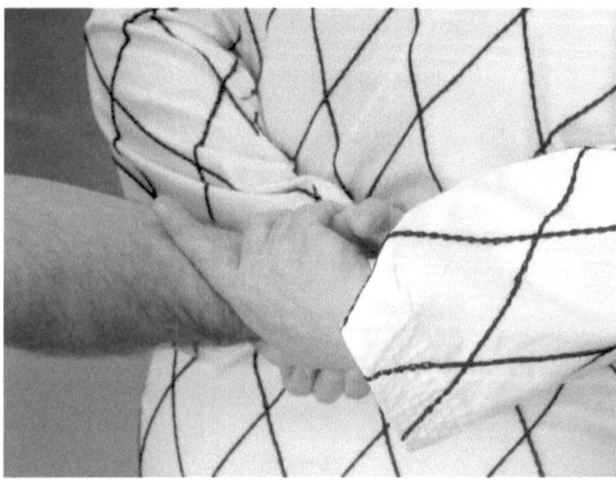

Figure 13: Clamshell lock

The Shoulder

Shoulder manipulations are slightly trickier than wrist manipulations due to size of the joint itself and the work necessary to get in a position to actually manipulate the joint. There is also a large muscle group protecting the shoulder making it difficult to manipulate the shoulder away from the chest with any success. The main points to remember in a shoulder manipulation are to get in tight and attempt to over rotate the shoulder backward and then back forward in a circular motion.

Figure 14: Shoulder moving toward an over-rotation situation

This has the best chance of causing pain and discomfort. Figure 14 shows a basic shoulder rotation with the arm being rotated out for an eventual lock.

There are three shoulder manipulations that we will use in this text. They are as follows:

Basic Chicken Wing – Figure 15

- Bring the opponent's arm across the opponent's back. Keep tight to the back with your hand controlling the arm at the opponent's hand.
- The opponent's forearm will initially start parallel to the ground.
- The opponent's upper arm will be perpendicular to the ground.
- Grab at the wrist and move the forearm from parallel to perpendicular to apply pressure upward. You are basically trying to touch their head with their own hand.
- Keep the arm tight to the opponent's back.

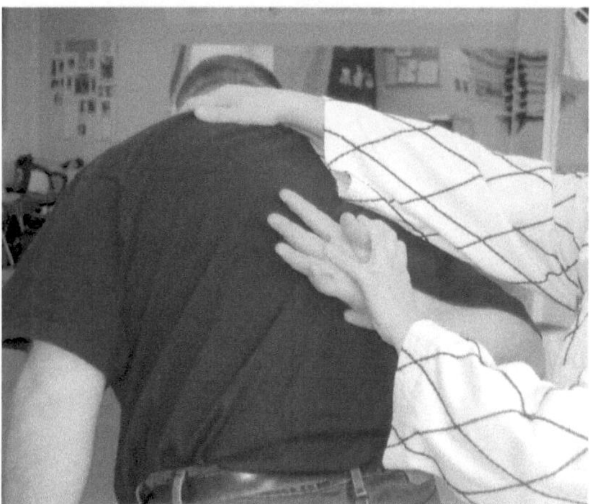

Figure 15: Basic chicken wing

Inter-twined Chicken Wing – Figure 16

- Technique will begin with opponent grapping the same side arm at the wrist.
- Grab the forearm at the pressure point of the holding hand right below the elbow crease. Grabbing at the elbow crease itself will work also for the technique, but will not cause the initial bit of pain the pressure point will.
- Push the held arm backwards and then move around the opponent, keeping the arm tight to the opponent's body.
- Your arm will then be inter-twined across the opponent's bicep and under their elbow.
- Keep tight and lift to apply pressure.

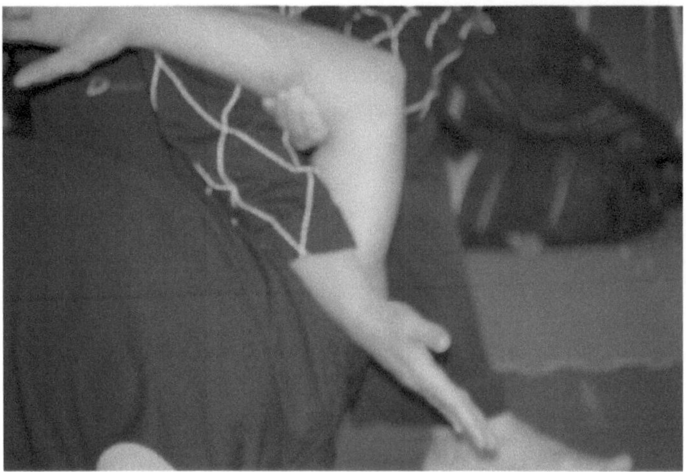

Figure 16: Inter-twined chicken wing

Triangle Shoulder Lock – Figure 17

- Grab the opponent at the lower portion of the bicep.
- Pull the bicep downward which will create a triangle of the opponent's arm. Trap the opponent's hand under the arm and keep tight.
- Place the other arm underneath the triangle created by the opponent's elbow bending and use this arm as a lever to apply pressure. Pull upward to apply pressure.

Figure 17: Triangle shoulder lock

The Elbow

The elbow has a definite forward and backward direction it wants to move, the direction opposite the elbow itself. There is very little side to side play in an elbow joint.

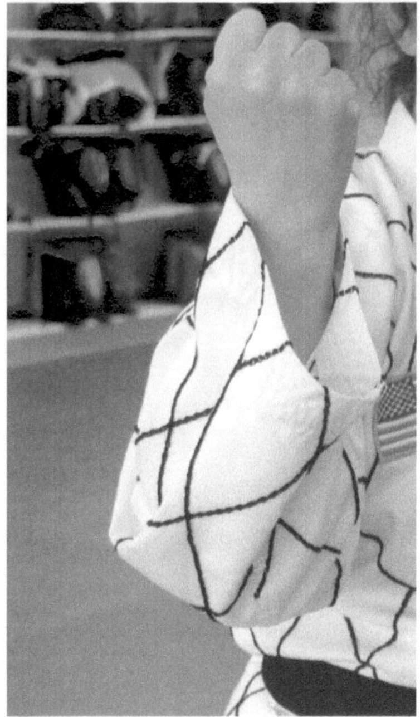

Figure 18: Elbow rotation forward and back

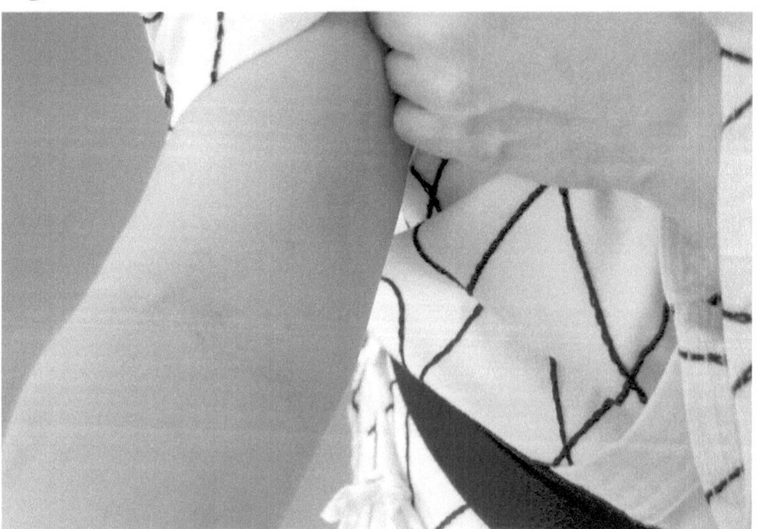

Figure 19: Elbow rotation side to side

The elbow is stressed in a joint manipulation scenario by barring out the elbow, effectively trapping it in a fully extended position and starting to move the arm in the direction away from the natural bend. If done fully this can cause elbow dislocation and breakage. Figure 20 shows the basic arm bar position with the arm fully extended and the opponent's wrist being bent backward and controlled by one hand. The other hand will put pressure down on the elbow joint itself while the opponent's arm is lifted.

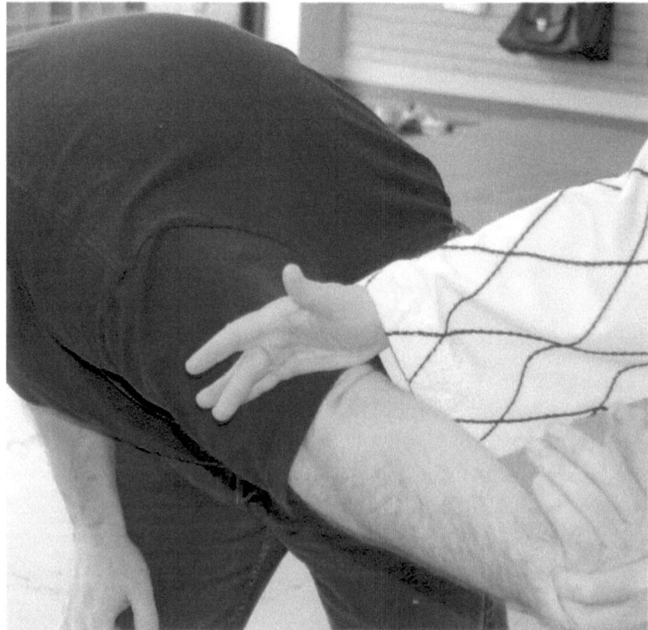

Figure 20: Basic arm bar

The method to secure the elbow in the position changes depending on the strength of the opponent and the beginning point of the sequence. There are four main arm bar variations that we will concentrate on in this text.

Inside Control Arm Bar – Figure 21

- Utilize a large circle to rotate the opponent's arm outward away from the body.
- The opponent's arm will rest on the top of your forward shoulder with their thumb pointing downward closest to your shoulder.

- Place both hands at the opponent's elbow and put pressure downward to cause pain. The will work against the upward movement of the arm at the wrist which is resting on your shoulder.

Figure 21: Inside control arm bar

Outside Control Arm Bar – Figure 22

- Rotate the opponent's arm to a locked out position while stepping to the outside of the opponent perpendicular to the opponent.
- Wrist control is important for the rotation and to keep the arm locked out. This is done by grabbing the opponent's hand around the fingers wrapping around the hand to the back. Then the wrist can be manipulated upward to lock it out.
- Lock out the arm and put pressure down at the elbow.

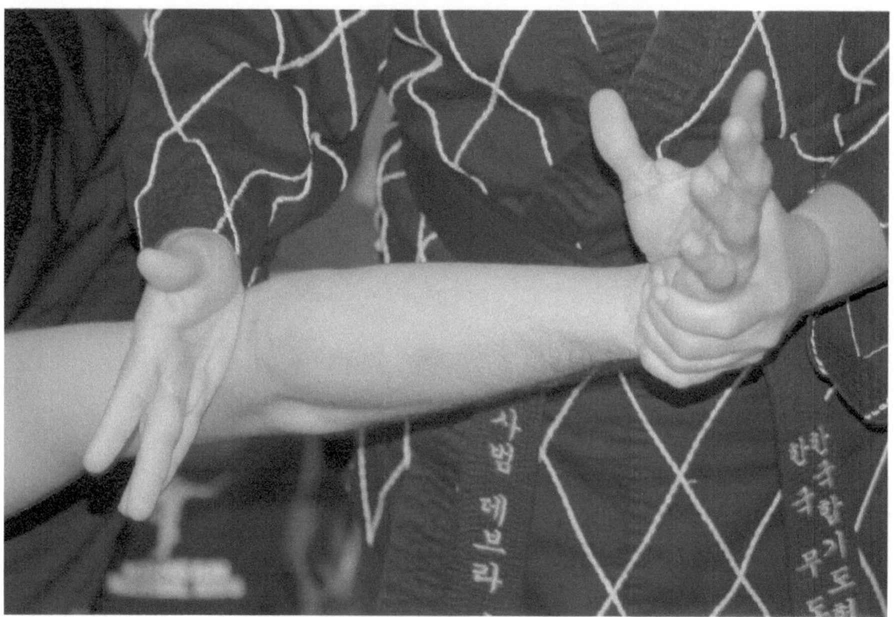

Figure 22: Outside control arm bar

Tight Outside Control Arm Bar – Figure 23

- This arm bar is utilized when you feel you need added leverage for control of the opponent's arm. This is gained by bringing the opponent's arm in tighter.
- Bring the arm up to place pressure on arm.
- Get opponent's elbow under you arm pit and clamp down tight.
- Lift arm up to apply pressure on elbow.

Figure 23: Transition to tight outside control arm bar

Upward Pressure Arm Bar – Figure 24

- Move to the outside of the opponent and wrap under the opponent's arm at the elbow.
- Elbow will be locked out and the pressure is generated by raising the wrapping arm upward.

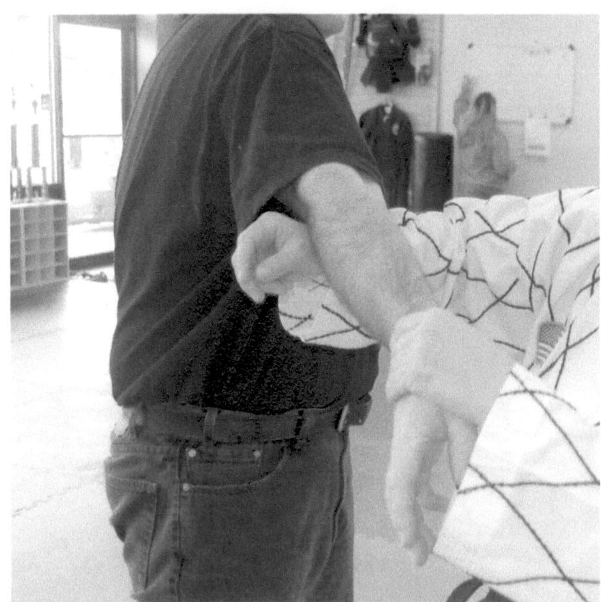

Figure 24: Upward pressure arm bar

Technique Chaining

Technique Chaining

In the last section we looked at individual techniques that target certain portions of the anatomy. Applying the initial technique itself is not always the end game, however. In this section we look at grouping those techniques together or what I call chaining.

The key to the application of any of the techniques shown is speed in technique and going with the force that the opponent's is generating. Go with the flow to the path of least resistance. When the opponent begins to resist the technique being applied before it has been applied fully and is effective, it is some time best to flow to another technique along the path of resistance. In essence, we chain one technique upon another until we get the desired results.

The practitioner will find which techniques tend to flow best for them and which apply best in certain situations. You will have your own favorite technique that you will go to in the majority of situations. My own favorites are either an outside arm bar or inside the opponent to a wrist lock if I can get a good grip on the thumb joint for leverage. I have found also which techniques flow the best for me from these techniques.

An arm bar that is being resisted toward the opponent can turn into a takedown by going with the resistance and changing the grip on the hand so the fingers now point toward the opponent. A step toward the opponent and this motion on the arm will normally cause the opponent to have to back break fall. If this does not cause the desired affect, a sweep can be applied as you are moving toward the opponent. This is shown in Figures 25 and 26. After the hand position is changed the wrist is locked out and you can proceed to the sweep or just retain the opponent here as shown in Figure 27.

Figure 25: Arm bar is applied

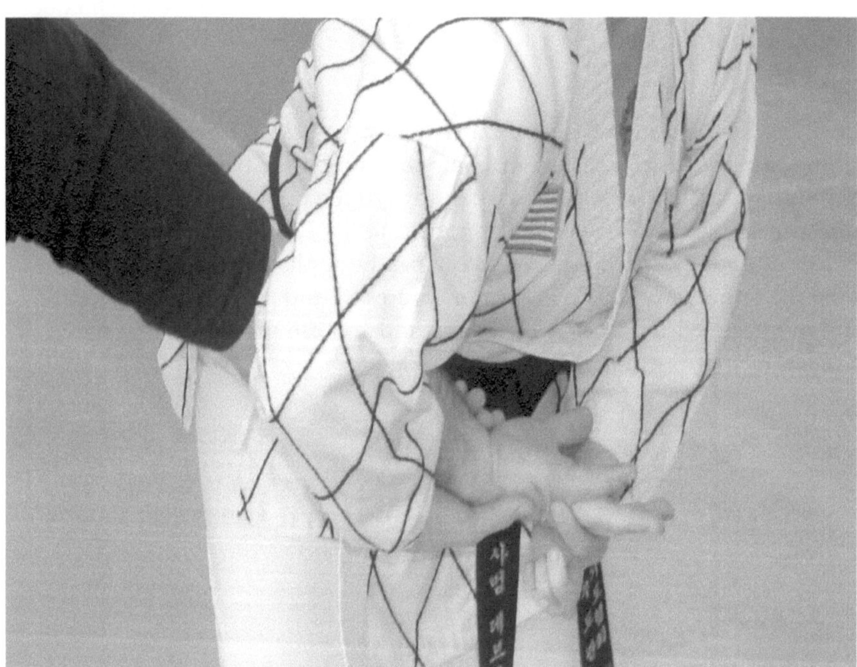

Figure 26: Hand position is changed to move to wrist lock

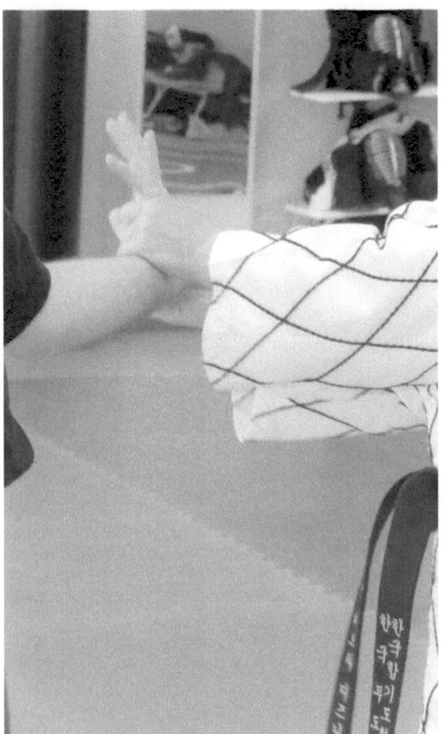

Figure 27: Wrist lock is applied

A wrist lock as shown in Figure 28 that is being resisted against the necessary lock rotation can be turned into an arm bar by going with the resistance. Move the hand toward the opponent and then to the outside to the arm bar position. Lock the arm out at the elbow to finish as shown in Figure 29. Remember to keep control of the arm by keeping the wrist lock throughout the transition.

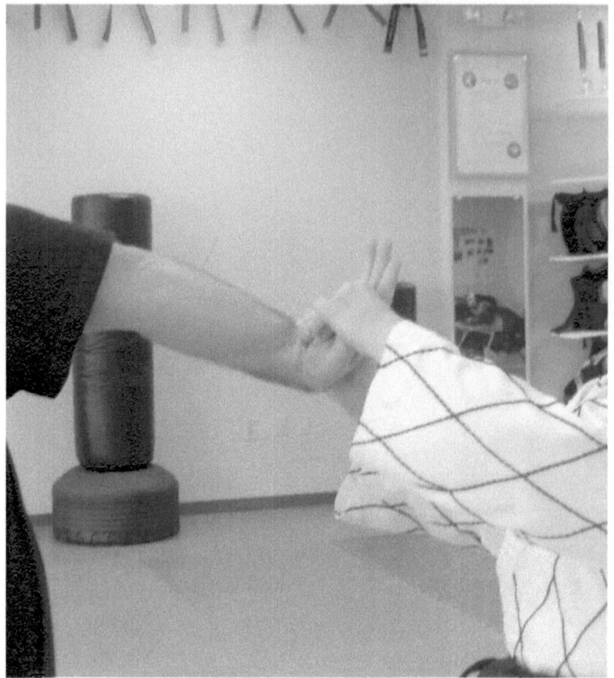

Figure 28: Initial wrist lock is applied

Figure 29: Hand is transitioned down to move to an arm bar

There are many more chaining opportunities you will find as you become more comfortable with the techniques. It is very important to work on the "what if" scenarios once you have the technique to a comfortable level in order to see what the various options are to re-apply the technique from another angle or to chain to a different technique that has a greater chance of success. This is my favorite part of the art, seeing what works and what doesn't. So experiment and see what you can come up with. We will give you the basic tools and you need to find out how they best work for you.

Technique Applications

Basic Techniques

Technique Listing

Technique Name: Wrist Manipulation, Basic

Technique Type: Joint Manipulation

Target: Wrist joint

Steps:

1. Start with in a fighting stance with your right leg back and your hands in front of you with the fingers open. Your opponent will have their left leg back in a fighting stance with their hands in front of them in fists.
2. Step with your right leg ending with right foot parallel with the opponent's lead leg. Grab lead hand with thumbs of both hands to rear of opponent's hand.
3. Turn hand to the outside of your opponent, keep your hand tight to the body at your chest level. This will allow you greater control of the opponent's hand as shown in Figure 30.
4. Step back and to the left and finish with pressure on the wrist with an outward rotation of the hand as shown in Figures 31 and 32. This move does not take a lot of force, just use leverage against the wrist and move smoothly.
5. Opponent will bend down if done lightly; side break fall if done moderately and somersault break fall if done fully.

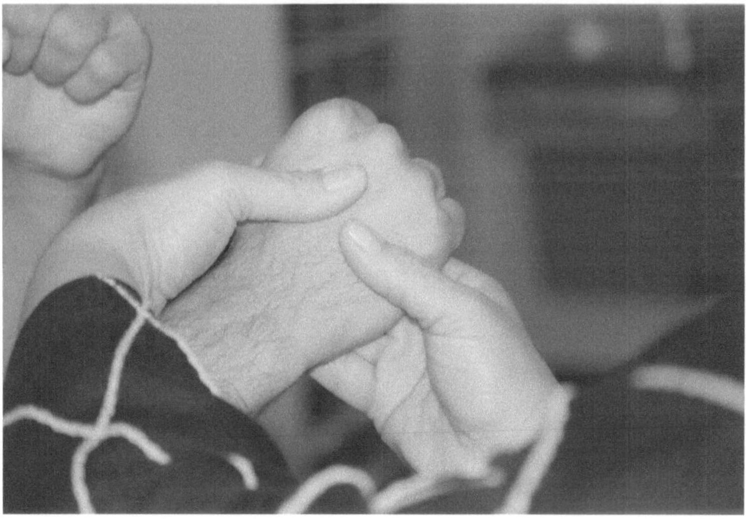

Figure 30: Grab with thumbs on back of hand

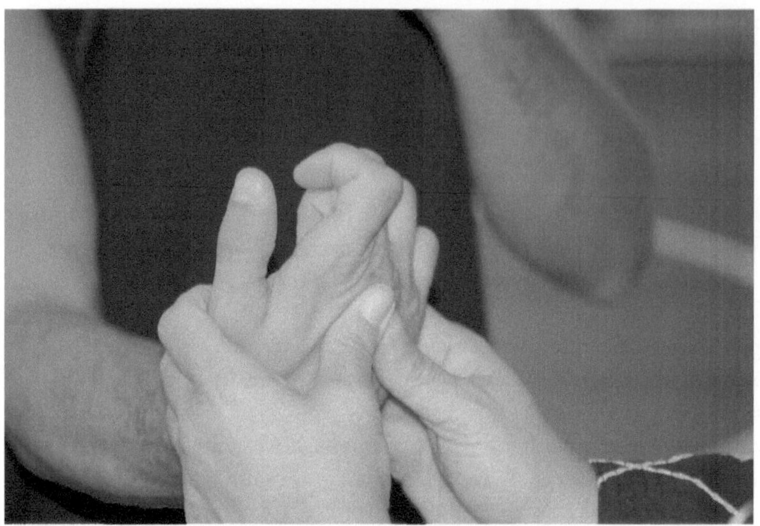

Figure 31: Initial outward rotation of hand

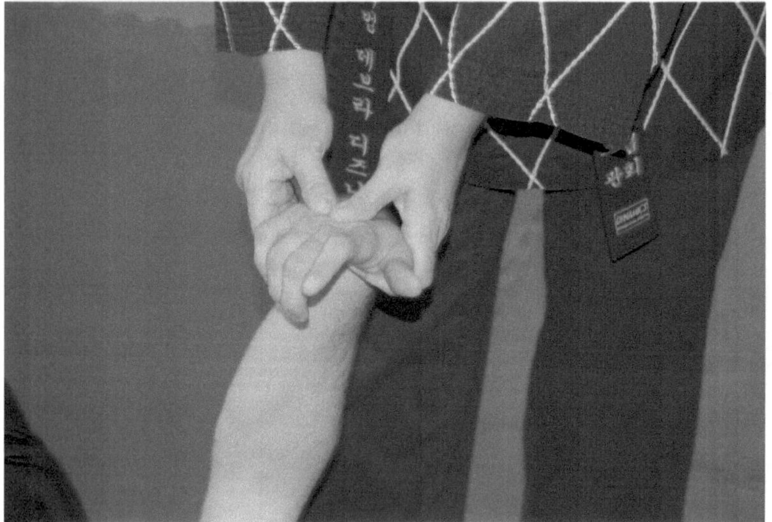

Figure 32: Finish with pressure

Notes:

This wrist manipulation had the thumb to the back of the opponent's hand and your fingers wrapped around the hand itself at the opponent's thumb. Use the thumb as a handle for the motion to allow you to move the wrist in the direction you want. You do not necessarily need to use the second hand to support the wrist lock, you can just use the grasping hand.

Technique Name: Basic Chicken Wing

Technique Type: Joint Manipulation

Target: Shoulder

Steps:

1. Start with your right leg back in a fighting stance with your hands in front of you with the fingers open. Opponent will have left leg back in a fighting stance with hands in front of them in fists.
2. Skip forward to the outside of the opponent's front foot, should be parallel to the opponent's lead leg. Grab the opponent's lead hand with the thumb to the top as shown in Figure 33.
3. Swing lead arm to the outside of the opponent. This will open a gap under the arm as shown in Figure 34.
4. Step though the gap and around to the back of the opponent.
5. Place held arm into a chicken wing, tight to the opponent's back as shown in Figure 35.
6. Grab the shoulder of the held arm. Curb kick to the rear leg at the opponent's knee. A curb kick is done by utilizing the knife blade of the foot in a downward motion. This is a low level kick and can be used to disrupt balance and cause pain to the leg area. This will cause the opponent to collapse to a knee.
7. Apply rear choke as opponent drops to knee as shown in Figure 36.

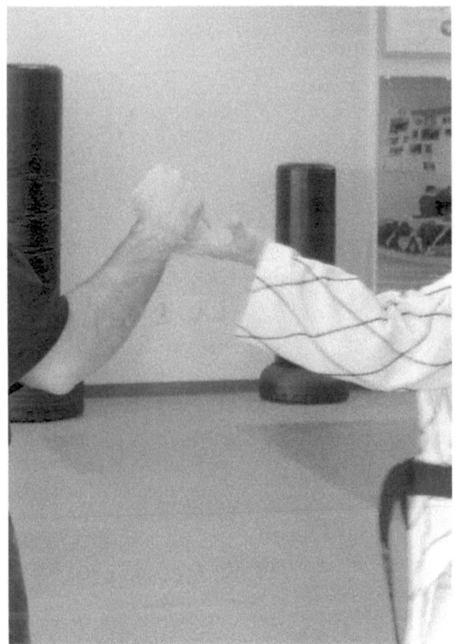

Figure 33: Initial grab for chicken wing

Figure 34: Turn around to the back of the opponent

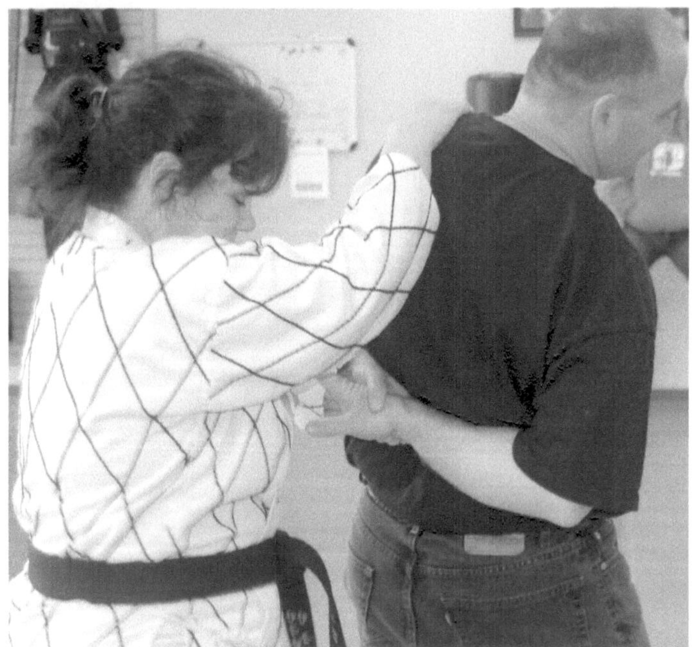

Figure 35: Lock in chicken wing and grab shoulder

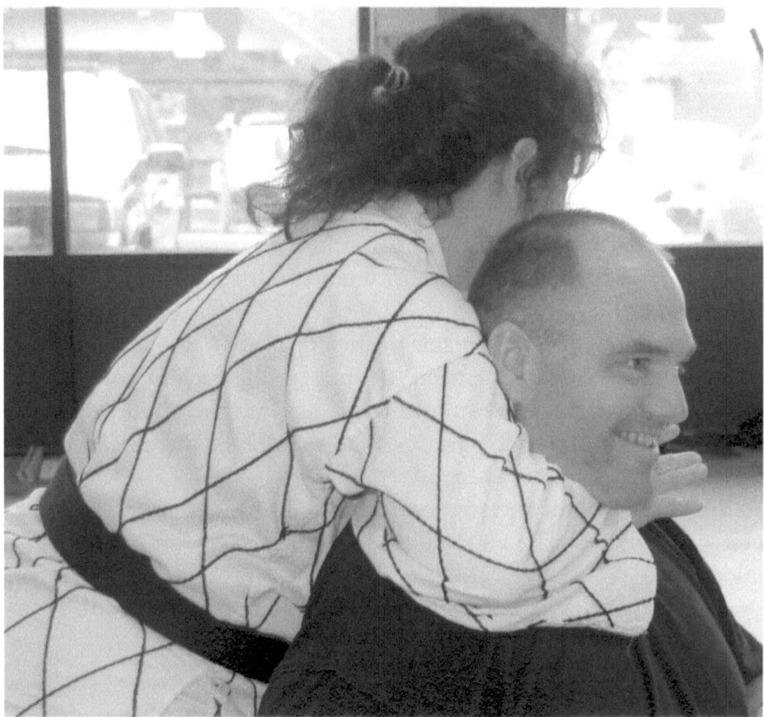

Figure 36: Finish with a choke

Notes:

The chicken wing should put pressure on the opponent's shoulder. Work the angle against the back to control pressure on the shoulder. The higher you lift the opponent's forearm, the more pressure is placed on the shoulder. Sharp movements upward will also cause increased stress on the opponent's shoulder.

Technique Name: Inside Control Arm Bar

Technique Type: Arm Bar

Target: Elbow

Steps:

1. Start with right leg back in a fighting stance with hands in front of you with your fingers open. Opponent will start with left leg back in a fighting stance with hands in front of them in a fist as shown in Figure 37.
2. Skip with the left leg to the outside of the opponent's lead leg.
3. Slap the inside of the opponent's lead arm with the back of your lead hand. Glide down the arm toward the wrist. Grab the opponent's wrist with your thumb to the inside of the wrist. Pull and extend the opponent's arm as shown in Figure 38.
4. Grab the lead shoulder and step back with right foot. Rotate the arm in a circular motion. The arm will finish resting on your forward shoulder.
5. Pressure down on the elbow joint, one inch about the elbow with two knife hands as shown in Figure 39

Figure 37: Starting position

Figure 38: Begin shoulder rotation

Figure 39: Finish with pressure at the elbow joint

Notes:

The larger the circle, the better. This rotation will cause the opponent to lean forward which facilitates the arm bar.

Technique Name: Outside Control Arm Bar

Technique Type: Arm Bar

Target: Elbow

Steps:

1. Opponent grabs the same side wrist. This is considered an outside wrist grab.
2. Open your held hand into live hand position to make room for the escape.
3. Grab opponent's holding hand with the free hand with your thumb placed at the space between the thumb and the forefinger. This is acupressure point four of the large intestine meridian as shown in Figure 40.
4. Rotate the holding arm outward with the arm straight as shown in Figure 41. Lock the arm out into an arm bar with opponent's elbow locked out. Use your held hand to rotate the shoulder to the outside by grasping the holding wrist.
5. Bring the held arm across the holding arm over the thumb and put pressure down with free hand while raising opponent's arm up as a lever as shown in Figure 42. Note when working with your partner lightly slide over the thumb.
6. Opponent kneels under light pressure; front break falls after being repositioned under more intense pressure.

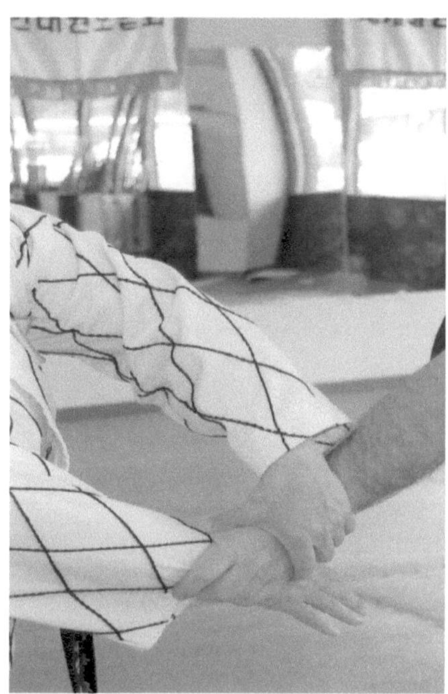

Figure 40: Grab opponent's hand to begin technique

Figure 41: Rotate arm over

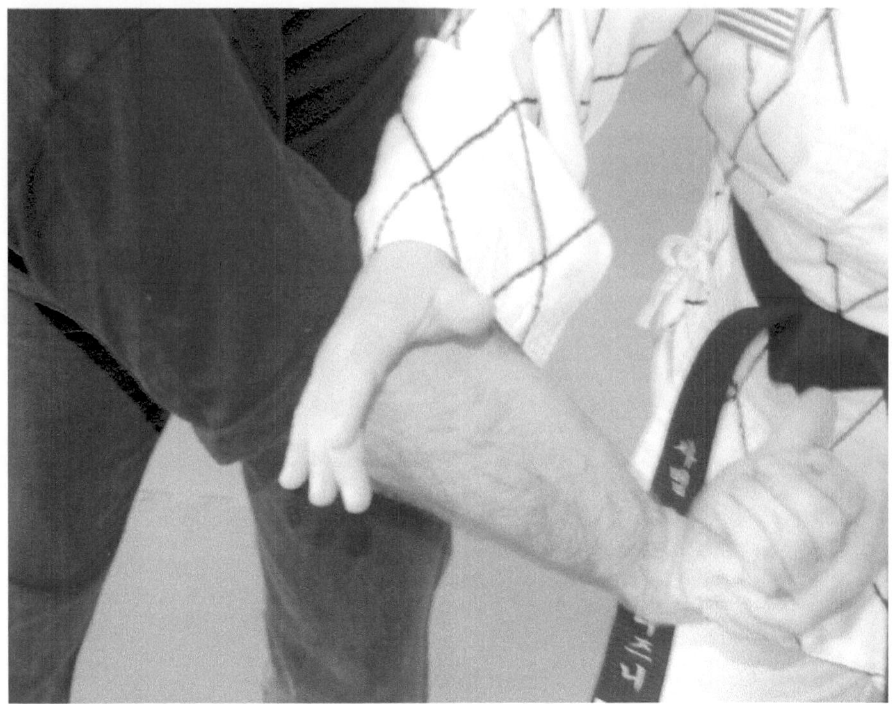

Figure 42: Finish with pressure at elbow

Notes:

The hand holding arm can also apply a wrist manipulation in the opposite direction of the pressure on the elbow.

Technique Name: Lateral Wrist Overextension

Technique Type: Joint Manipulation

Target: Wrist

Steps:

1. Technique begins from a clothing grab with the opponent grabbing at the bottom of the sleeve at the wrist.
2. Grab the holding hand with the free hand covering the holding hand tight to the wrist as shown in Figure 43.
3. Open hand into live hand and rotate held hand outward with your wrist directly on the opponent's. Make sure thumb side of wrist is facing the thumb side of the opponent's wrist. Break the grip at the thumb of the opponent. This is shown in Figure 44.
4. Push the opponent's arm out and step forward with the off leg to a perpendicular position to the opponent as shown in Figure 45. Opponent will slightly spin.
5. Opponent takes a back break fall if spun moderately, side break fall if spun more intensely. Follow opponent down to a knee.

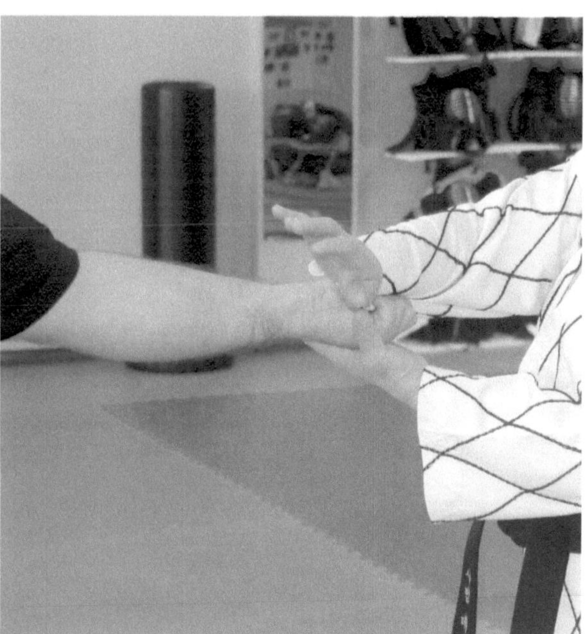

Figure 43: Grab holding hand and begin to rotate under holding arm

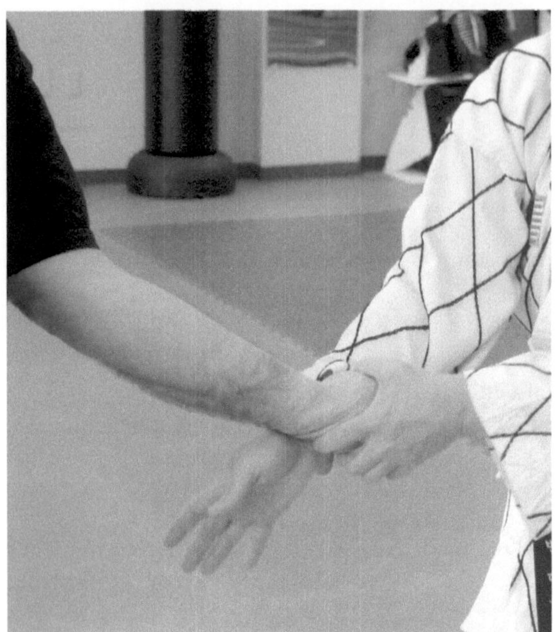

Figure 44: Rotation into opponent's wrist

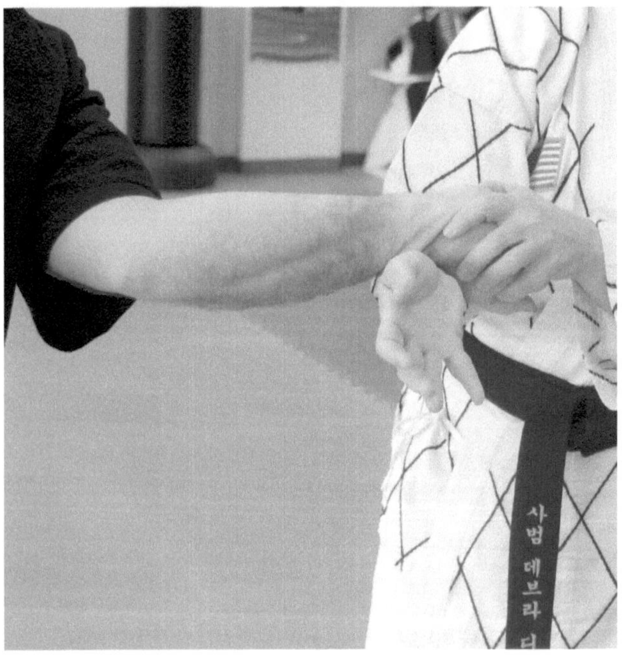

Figure 45: Finish with pressure

Technique Name: Vertical Pump Handle Wrist Lock

Technique Type: Joint Manipulation

Target: Wrist

Steps:

1. Technique begins with a clothing grab with opponent grabbing the front of the top at the bottom of the collar at the lapel.
2. Grab holding hand with right hand. Turn holding hand over with the right hand. Thumb is pointing downward as shown in Figure 46.
3. Grab near opponent's wrist with your left hand and rotate the holding hand until pinky side is facing up as shown in Figure 47.
4. Step forward and twist hand upward with left hand and wrist joint backward with the right as shown in Figure 48.
5. Step back and opponent front break falls or step forward and opponent drops to their knees.

Figure 46: Grab holding hand with thumb pointing downward

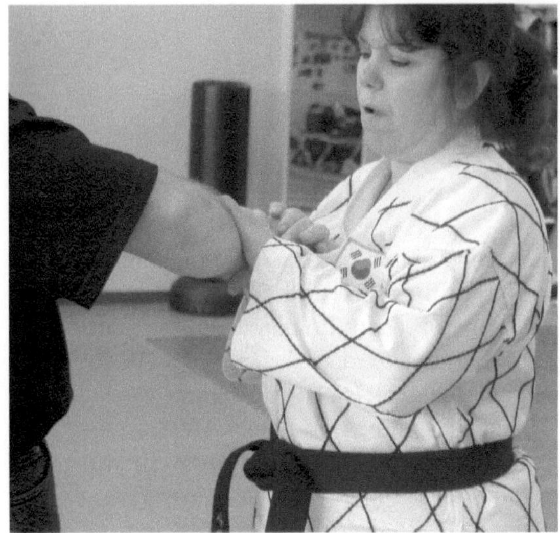

Figure 47: Rotate opponent's hand until pinky side is facing up

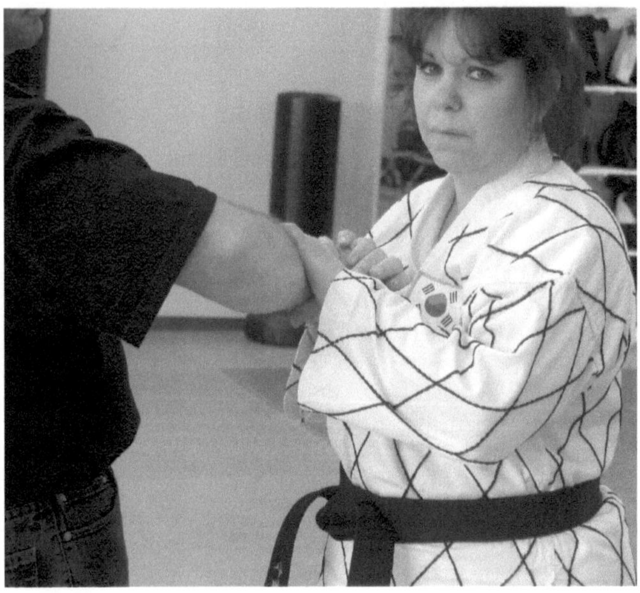

Figure 48: Finish with pressure

Notes:

The motion should be similar to a pump handle motion. It is like you are turning on a faucet, lifting upward and downward at the same time.

Technique Name: Wrist Manipulation Off an Inside Wrist Grab

Technique Type: Joint Manipulation

Target: Wrist

Steps:

1. Opponent performs an inside wrist grab, grabbing the opposite wrist.
2. Open hand into live hand to make room for the escape. Bring the held arm straight up with your elbow at 90 degrees, this will break the grip. This is shown in Figure 49.
3. Grab the holding hand with the off hand with your thumb to the back of the opponent's hand as shown in Figure 50.
4. Step forward and to the right to position yourself next to your opponent.
5. Step back to the left and put pressure down on the hand as shown in Figure 51. This performs the standard wrist manipulation.
6. Opponent will back break fall.

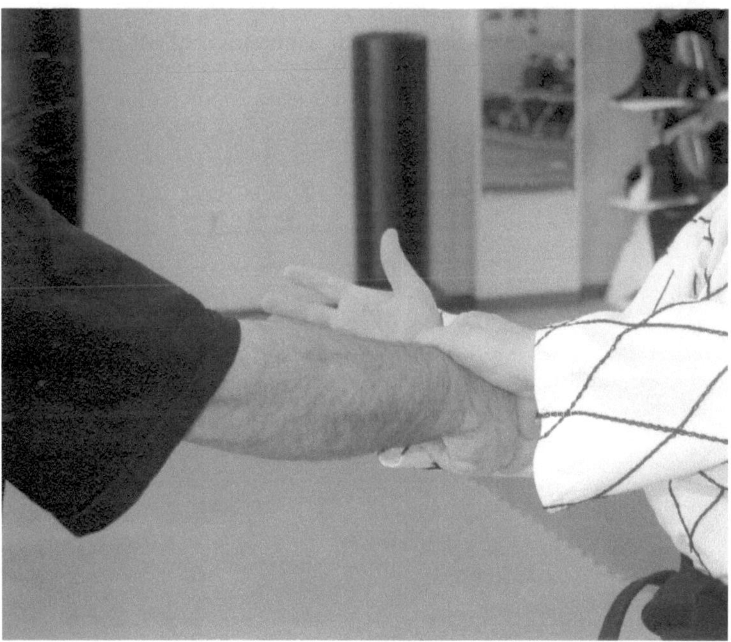

Figure 49: Initial grab and beginning of movement to enact wrist grab

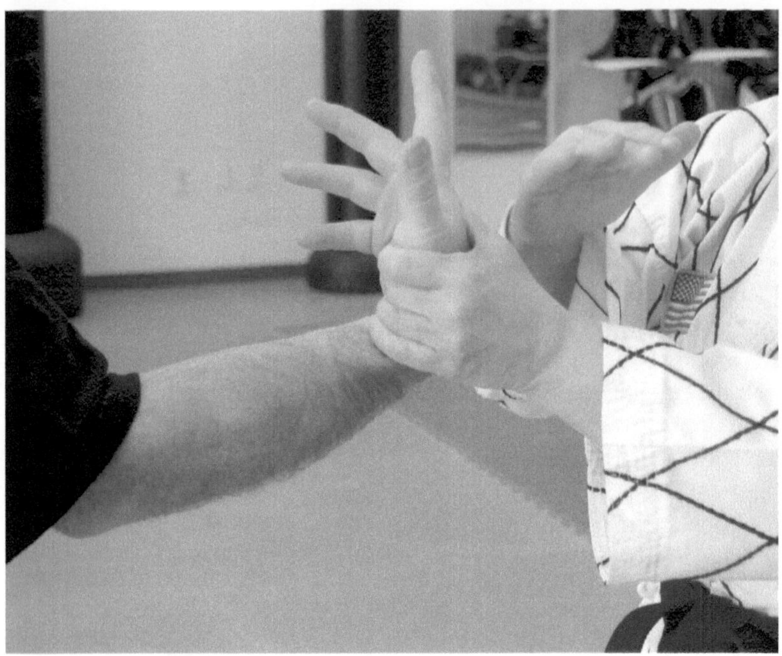

Figure 50: Apply pressure to rear of hand with assistance of off hand

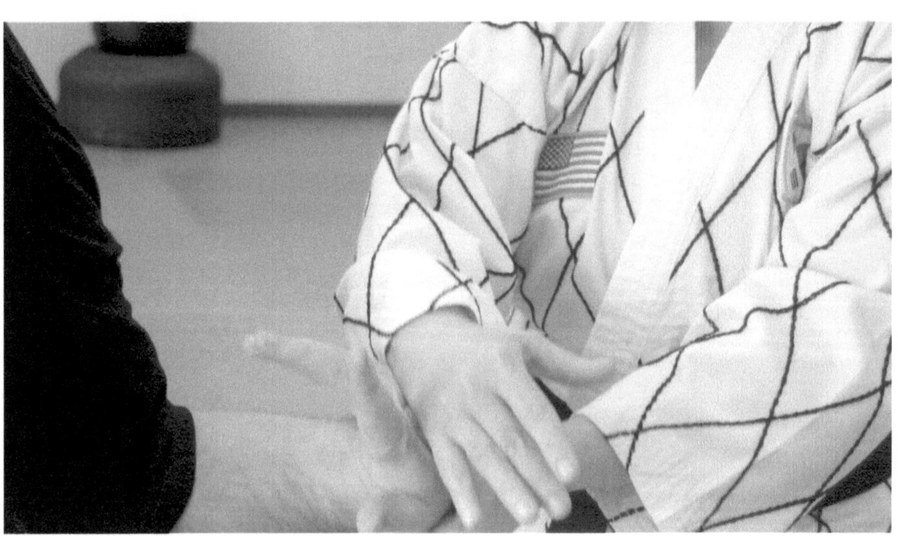

Figure 51: Finish with pressure

Technique Name: Elbow Dislocation with Bump

Technique Type: Joint Manipulation

Target: Elbow

Steps:

1. Opponent performs an inside wrist grab, grabbing the right wrist with both hands as shown in Figure 52.
2. Right hand grabs the inside wrist of the opponent's right arm to secure it.
3. Left foot steps forward sideways to opponent with left leg next to right leg of opponent.
4. Left bicep bumps the opponent's right tricep as shown in Figure 53. The right hand will pull both arms forward at the same time.
5. Left hand grabs either in between opponent's arms to the right wrist or wraps around both wrists as shown in Figure 54.
6. Right foot steps backwards so you are facing the same direction as the opponent.
7. Fold forward with the left shoulder, breaking the opponent's right elbow.

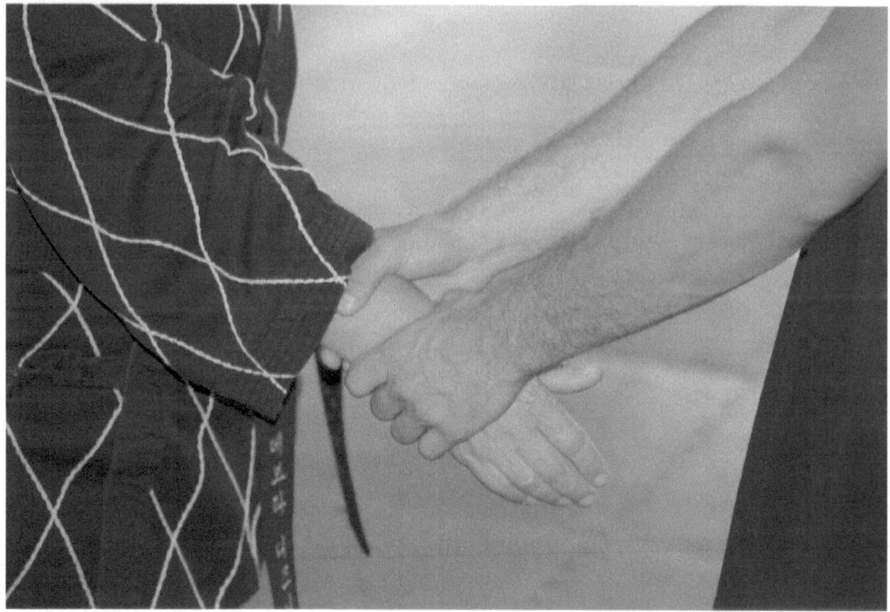

Figure 52: Opponent grabs right wrist with both hands

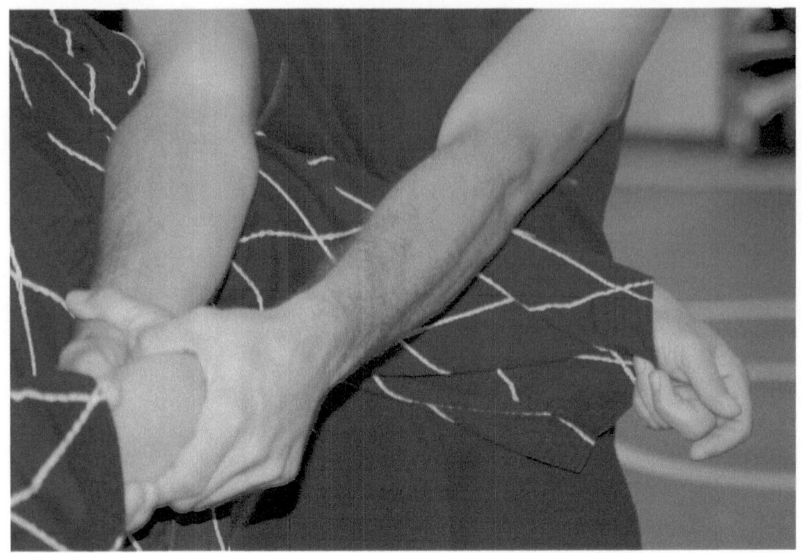

Figure 53: Left bicep bumps right tricep

Figure 54: Finish with shoulder folding forward

Intermediate Techniques

Technique Listing

Technique Name: Outside Wrist Grab Manipulation

Technique Type: Joint Manipulation

Target: Wrist

Steps:

1. Opponent grabs same arm at the wrist. This is considered an outside wrist grab.
2. Open held hand in live hand position to make room for the escape as shown in Figure 55.
3. Rotate the held hand upward with the palm on the held hand facing toward your chest as shown in Figure 56.
4. Grab opponent's holding hand with the free hand, thumb between the knuckles of the back of the opponent's hand. Place fingers around the thumb.
5. Push out the held hand toward the wrist and move the held hand to the right as shown in Figure 57. Step forward with a right step.
6. Place pressure on the holding hand with a knife hand using the off hand as shown in Figure 58.
7. Opponent bends down under light pressure; side break falls under moderate pressure and somersault break falls under high pressure.

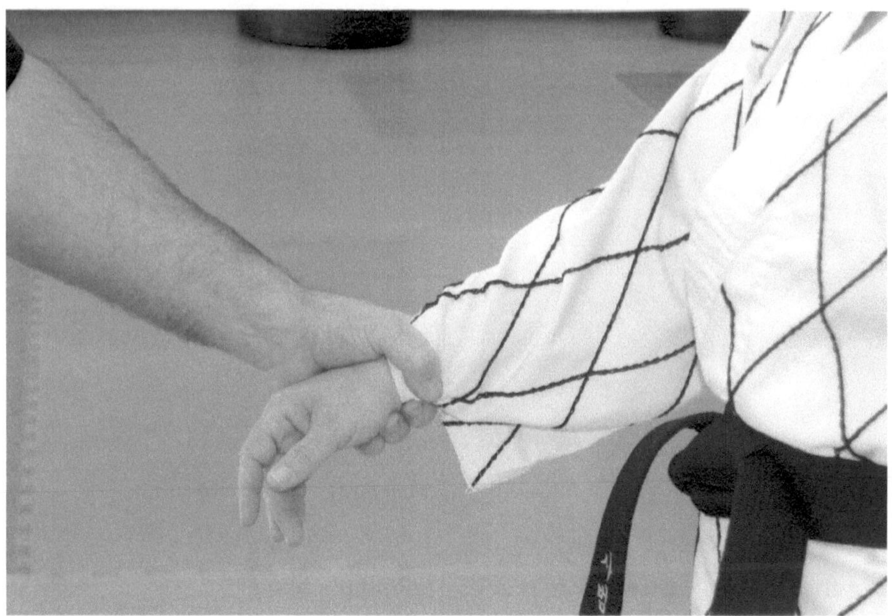

Figure 55: Beginning of technique

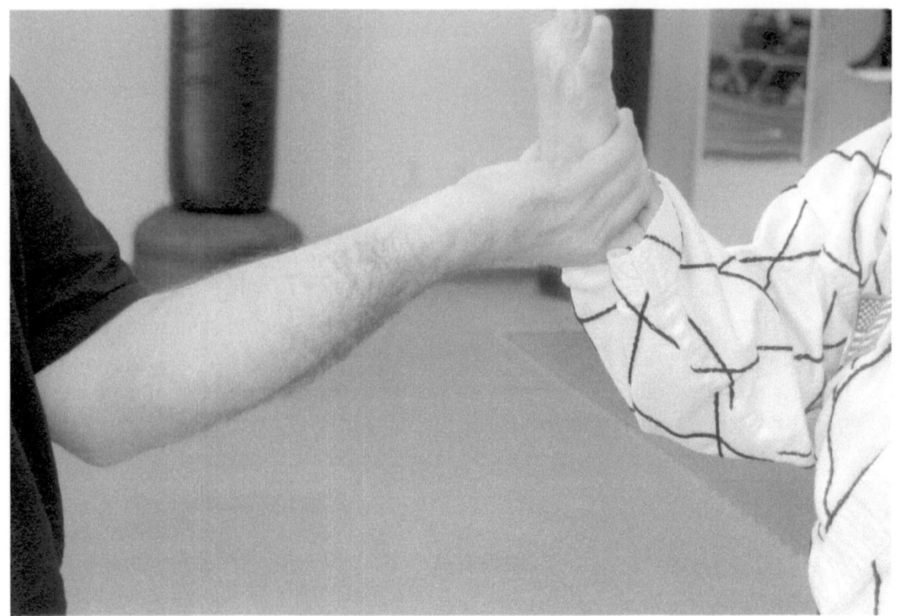

Figure 56: Rotate hand upward facing your chest

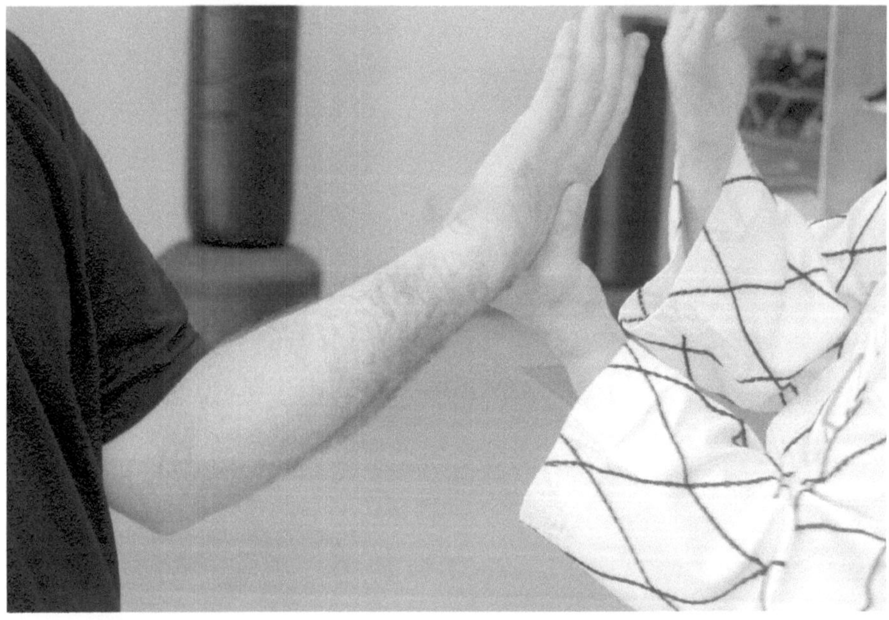

Figure 57: Apply pressure to rear of opponent's hand

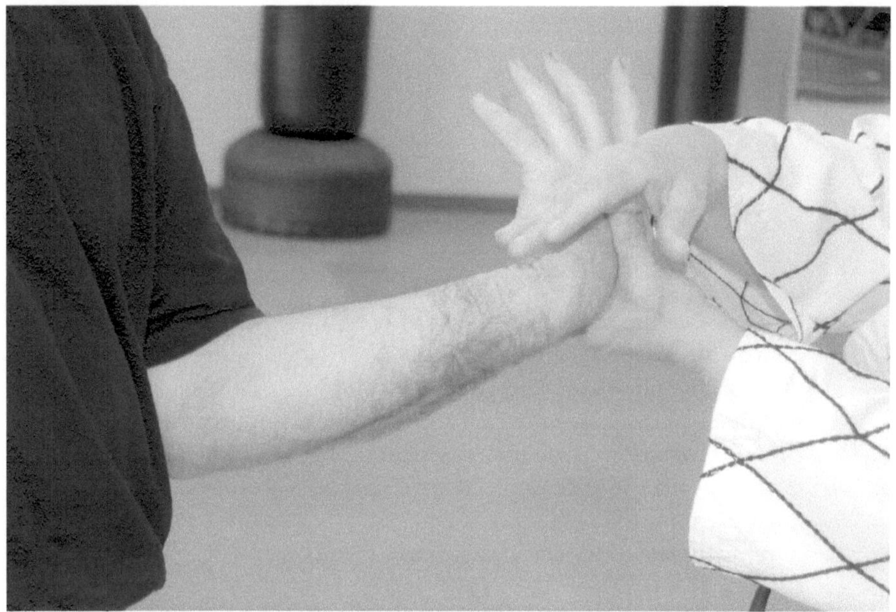

Figure 58: Finish with pressure from off hand

Notes:

This technique again uses the thumb joint as the handle for the wrist manipulation. Make sure to reach around the holding hand to grab, actually reach under the hand.

Technique Name: Triangle Shoulder Lock

Technique Type: Joint Manipulation

Target: Shoulder

Steps:

1. Technique begins with clothing grab with the opponent grabbing the underneath of the sleeve at the bicep.
2. Grab across the opponent's body to the bottom sleeve of the holding arm at the bicep as shown in Figure 59. You will mirror the opponent's grab on the same arm with your off arm.
3. Shoot held arm above the crook of the elbow to the outside of the arms. This will collapse the opponent's elbow as shown in Figure 60.
4. Step forward and pull arm to chest. Grab opponent's hand and apply pressure upward as shown in Figure 61.
5. Opponent will move until back break falling.

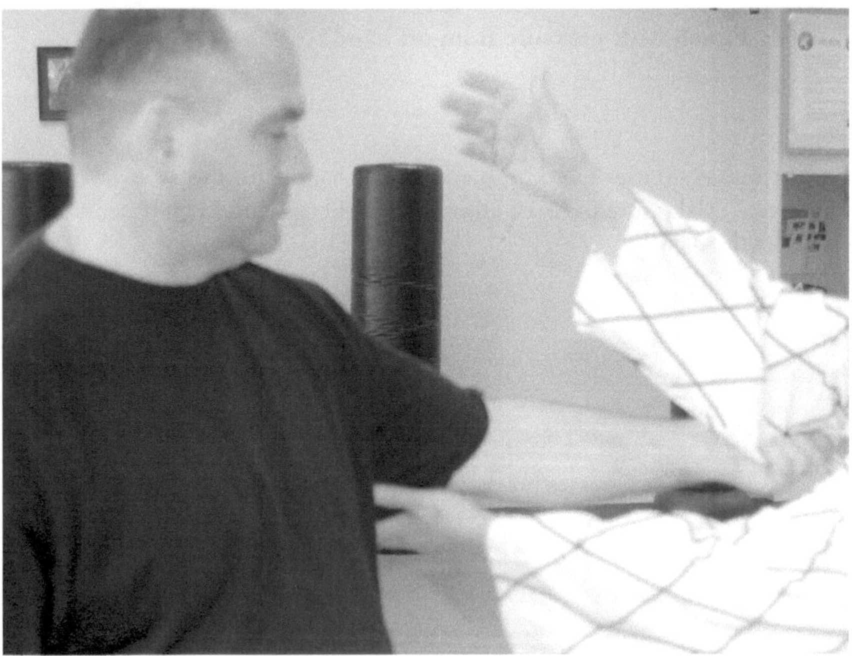

Figure 59: Grab across to opponent's bottom sleeve and begin to shoot arm through

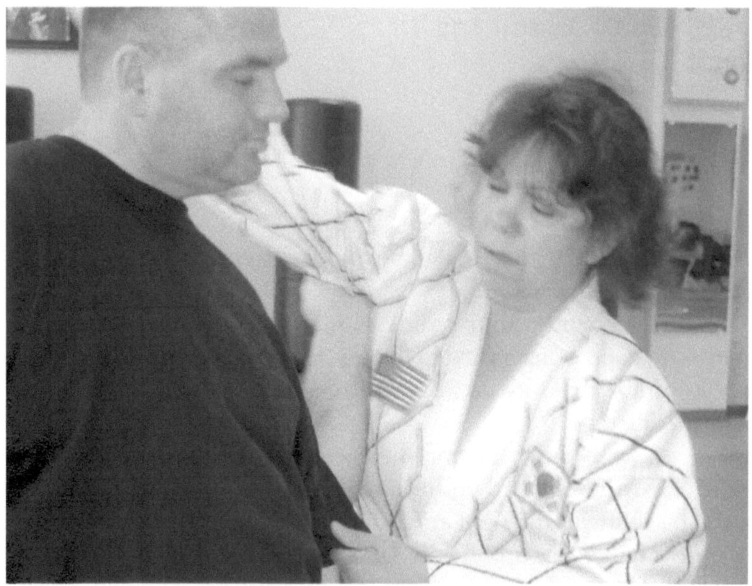

Figure 60: Collapse elbow and rotate parallel to opponent

Figure 61: Finish with upward pressure

Notes:

Apply upward pressure to increase the pain of the shoulder lock.

Technique Name: Arm Pit Assisted Arm Bar

Technique Type: Arm Bar

Target: Elbow

Steps:

1. Technique will begin with a hair grab with opponent grabbing the top of the head facing toward you.
2. Grab the holding hand with the same hand. Cover the top of the hand with opposite hand using a claw hand grip to secure hand as shown in Figure 62. Utilize pressure point at acupressure point four of the large intestine meridian.
3. Place the same arm under the opponent's arm at the elbow at a 90 degree angle. Arms will end up flush together with forearms flush.
4. Twist torso slightly to the right and put pressure on opponent's wrist, which is now pinky side up. At the same time come over top of opponent's arm with the left elbow to put pressure on the elbow joint as shown in Figure 63.
5. Opponent will bend forward.
6. Opponent will tap with moderate pressure and break fall with more intense pressure.

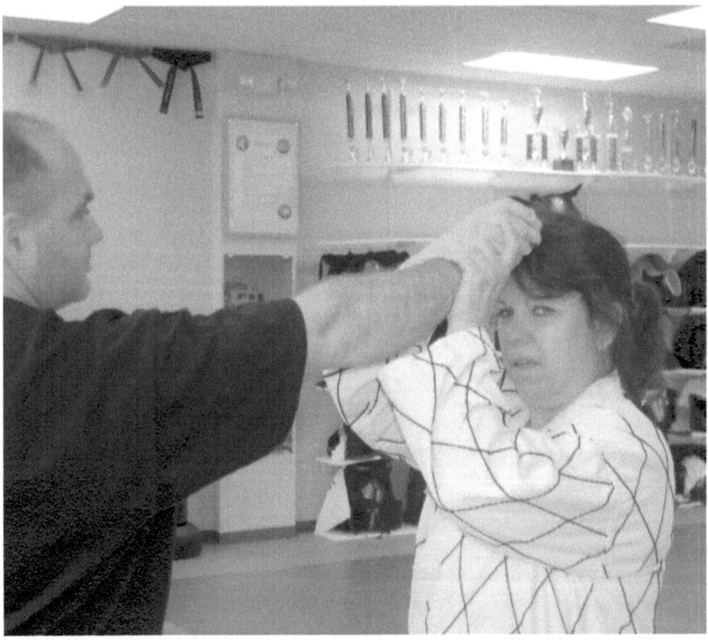

Figure 62: Begin with opponent grabbing front of hair

Figure 63: Turn and lock opponent's arm under your arm pit

Notes:

Arm bar is controlled under the arm pit to give more leverage to the lock.

Technique Name: Momentum Flow Wrist Lock

Technique Type: Joint Manipulation

Target: Wrist

Steps:

1. Technique begins from a clothing grab with the opponent grabbing the front of the person and then pushing them backward as shown in Figure 64.
2. Go with the push and yield, move to the outside of the push.
3. Grab the pushing hand with the thumb to the outside (back) of the hand as shown in Figure 65. This is the standard wrist manipulation position.
4. Step back and out, bring pressure down on the wrist as shown in Figure 66.
5. Opponent will side break fall when the technique is done at moderate speed. Opponent will somersault break fall when the technique is done at a higher speed.

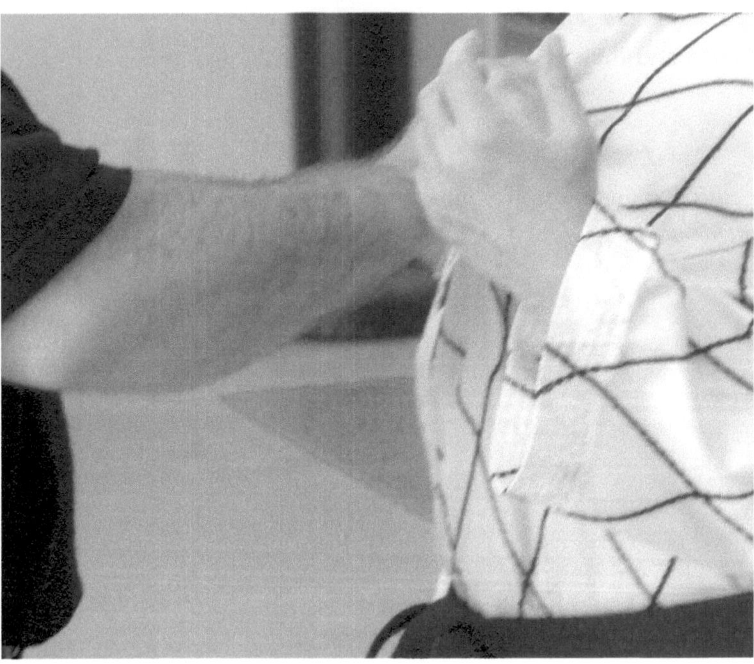

Figure 64: Beginning clothing grab

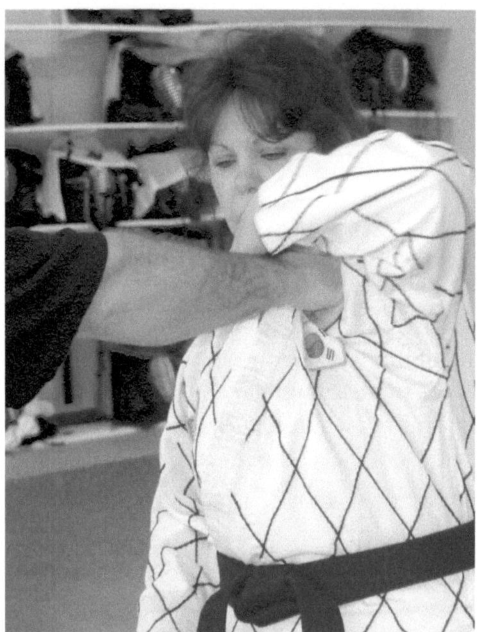

Figure 65: Begin to peel hand off your clothing

Figure 66: Finish with pressure on back of hand

Notes:

The end is the standard wrist manipulation; you go with the flow of the push to the inside of the opponent to apply technique.

Use the opponent's momentum to increase the pressure on the wrist.

Technique Name: Momentum Flow Wrist Lock with Sweep

Technique Type: Joint Manipulation

Target: Wrist

Steps:

1. Technique begins from a clothing grab. Opponent grabs the front of the top and then pulls toward them as shown in Figure 67.
2. Yield with the pull and step forward toward the opponent.
3. Grab the pulling hand with the thumb to the outside (back) of the hand as shown in Figure 68. This is the standard wrist manipulation position. Apply pressure to wrist as shown in Figure 69.
4. Kick out opponent's lead leg with foot closest to it for a sweep. Opponent does a backward break fall.

Figure 67: Beginning of technique with clothing grab with a push

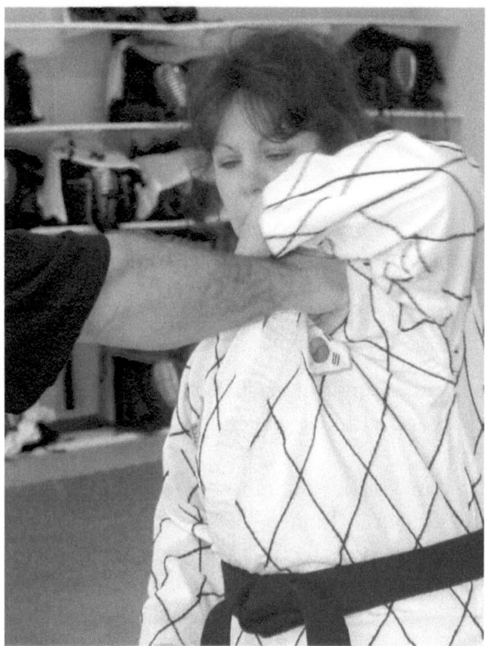

Figure 68: Turn and grab hand

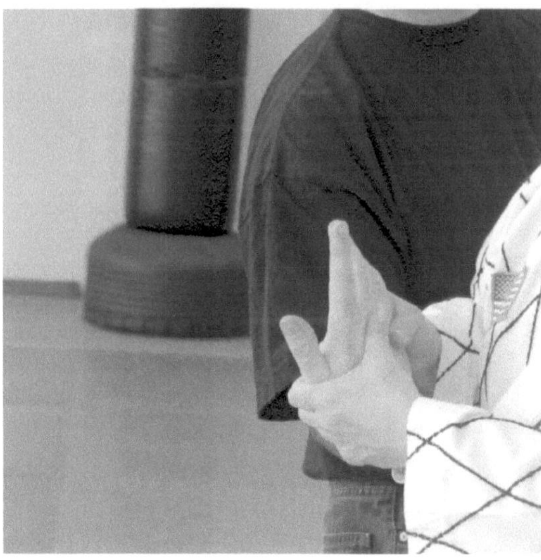

Figure 69: Finish with pressure

Notes:

It is important in this technique not to break the momentum supplied by your opponent. Go with the momentum and use it to help with the wrist manipulation and increase the intensity of the sweep.

Technique Name: Single Arm Trapping Arm Bar

Technique Type: Arm Bar

Target: Elbow

Steps:

1. Technique begins with a clothing grab with opponent grabbing the belt from over the top as shown in Figure 70.
2. Swing right arm under the opponent's arm and hook grabbing arm as shown in Figure 71.
3. Bring hand up to chest, open hand facing out as shown in Figure 72.
4. Step left and in to make room to apply the arm bar. This will move the left leg to the opponent's right leg.
5. Pressure on elbow with a knife hand under the elbow and roll over the elbow above the elbow joint as shown in Figure 73.
6. Opponent kneels and taps to indicate an effective technique.

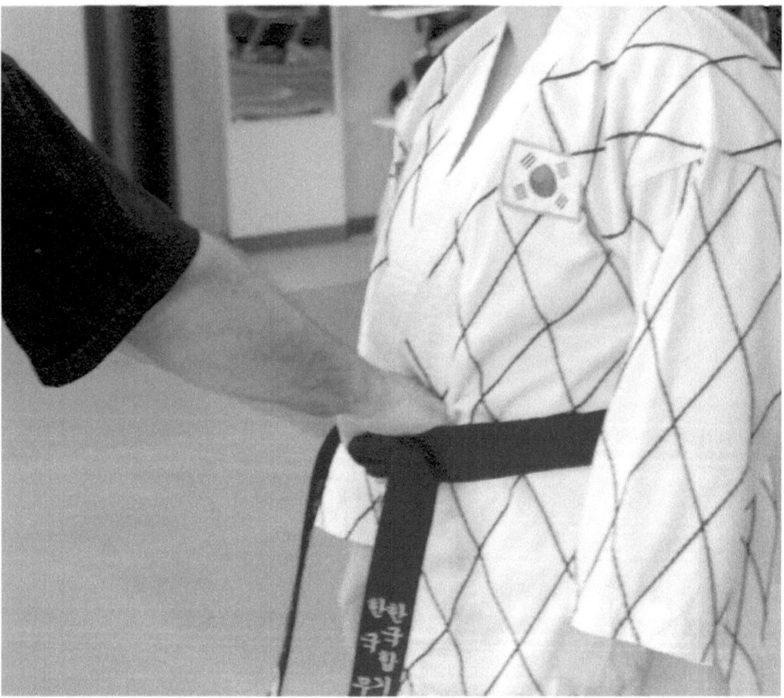

Figure 70: Initial grab over top of belt

Figure 71: Hook grabbing hand

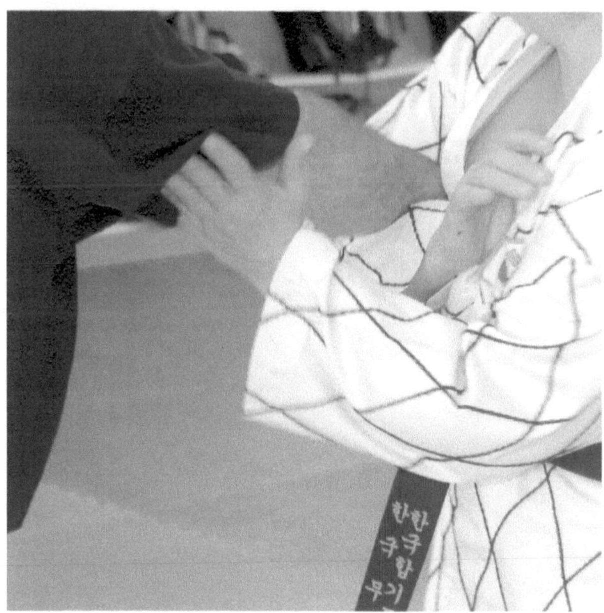

Figure 72: Begin to turn arm over into arm bar position

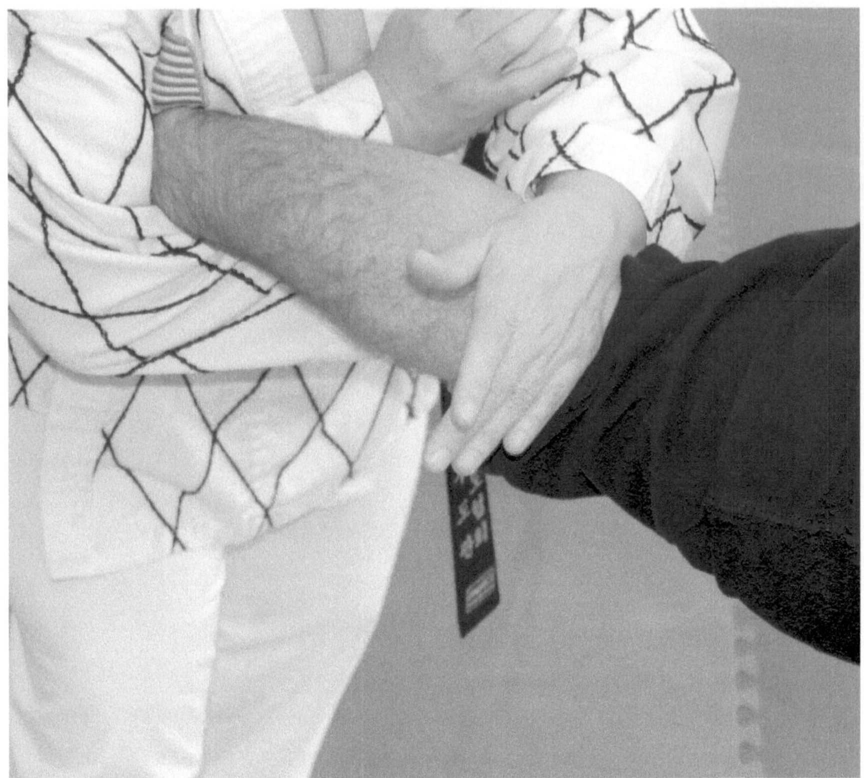

Figure 73: Finish in arm bar position, pressure at elbow

Notes:

Trap the holding hand to the belt.

Rotate over and around the elbow. Utilize the back of the forearm.

Technique Name: Wrapping Arm Bar

Technique Type: Arm Bar

Target: Elbow

Steps:

1. Opponent grabs from behind, grabbing the middle rear of the belt with one hand as shown in Figure 74.
2. Step back to the left with the body ending up parallel to the opponent.
3. Apply a knife strike to the opponent's throat.
4. Wrap the grasping arm at the elbow with the arm utilizing the elbow joint to trap the opponent's arm as shown in Figure 75.
5. Shift the shoulder to put pressure down on the elbow as shown in Figure 76 and step back as shown in Figure 77.
6. Opponent will do a front break fall.

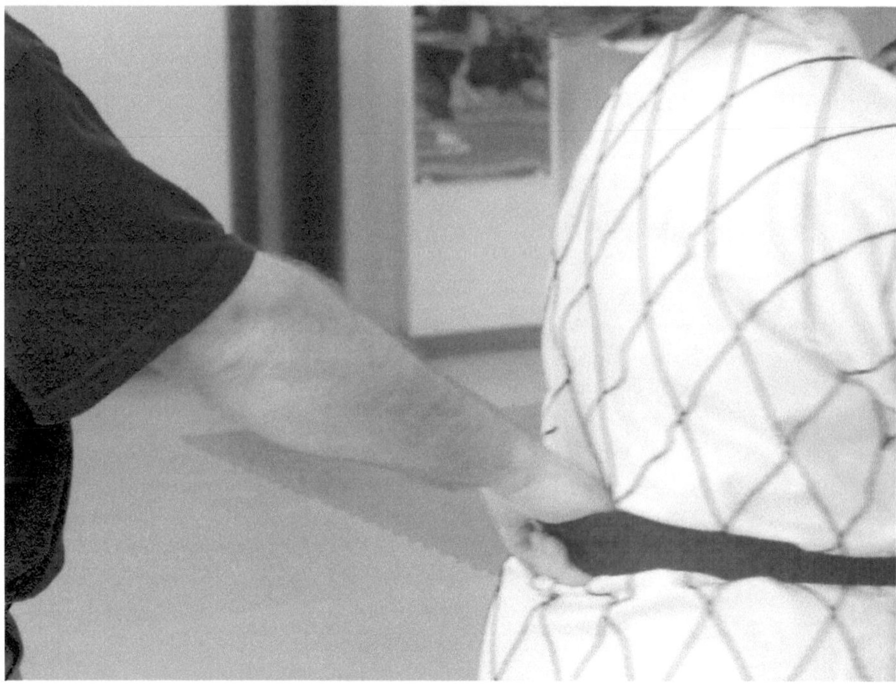

Figure 74: Initial grab for technique

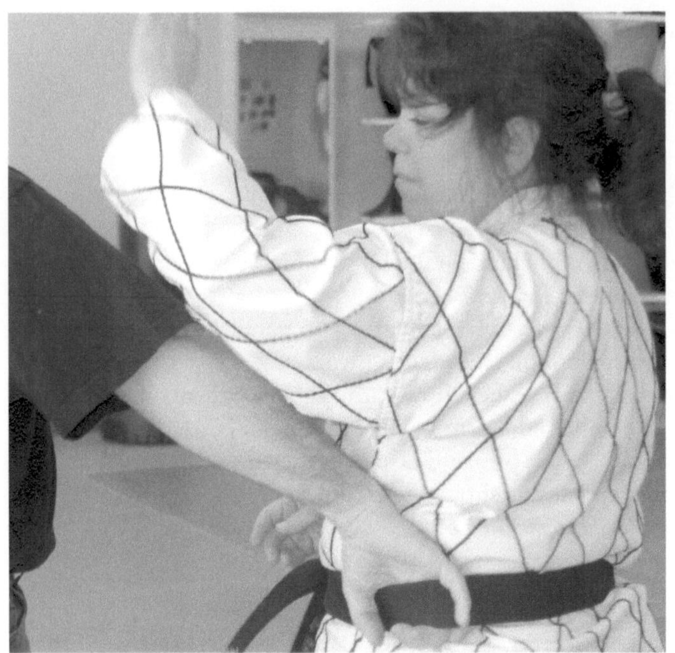

Figure 75: Arm wraps around at elbow to trap arm

Figure 76: Opponent's arm is trapped

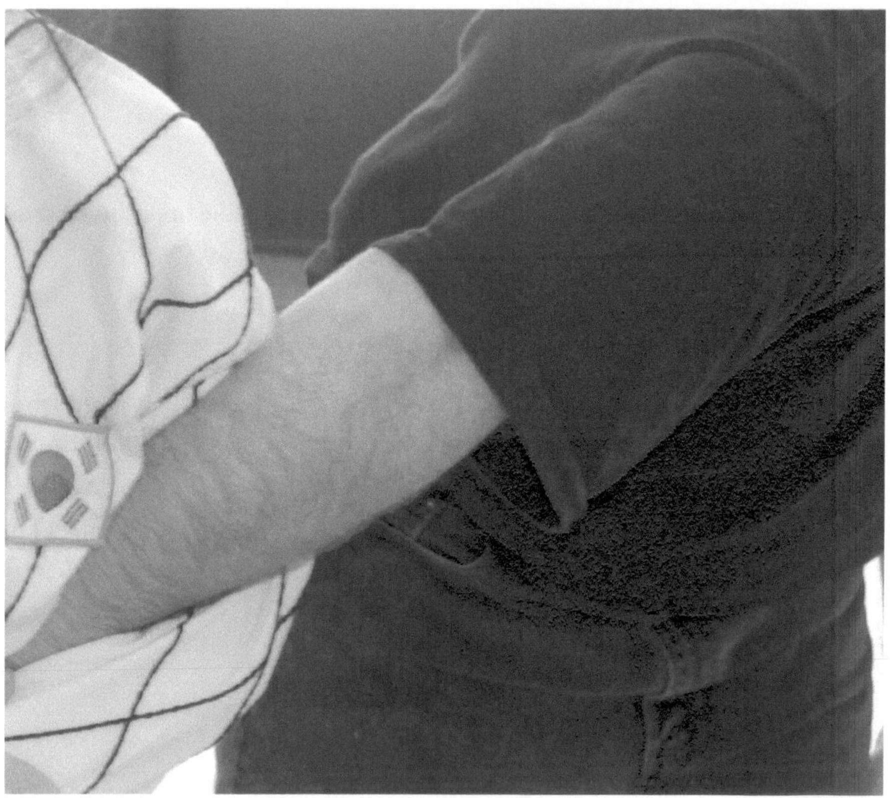

Figure 77: Shoulder shifts forward for finish

Technique Name: Wrist Manipulation Off an Inside Wrist Grab Number Two

Technique Type: Joint Manipulation

Target: Wrist

Steps:

1. Opponent performs an inside wrist grab, grabbing the opposite wrist as shown in Figure 78.
2. Open the held hand into live hand position with the fingers spread wide to make room.
3. Lower held hand to belt and grab holding hand over the back of the holding hand with off hand.
4. Rotate the held hand over the opponent's wrist as shown in Figure 79.
5. Get the wrist over the opponent's wrist with the heel of the held hand.
6. Rotate the held arm over and step forward. Place pressure downward on the wrist with the heel of the held hand as shown in Figure 80.
7. Opponent will drop to knees to signify a successful application of the technique.

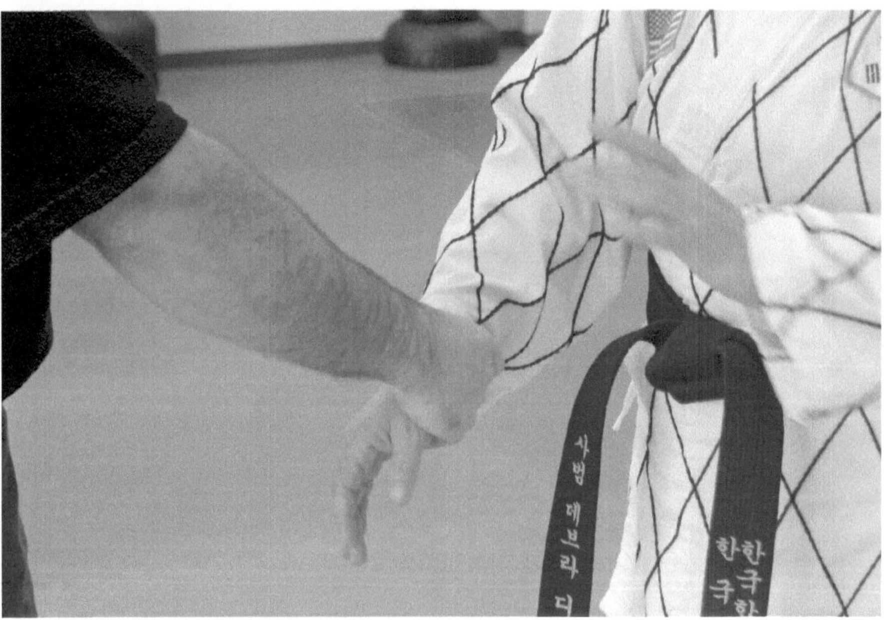

Figure 78: Initial grab

Figure 79: Hand rotates over held hand

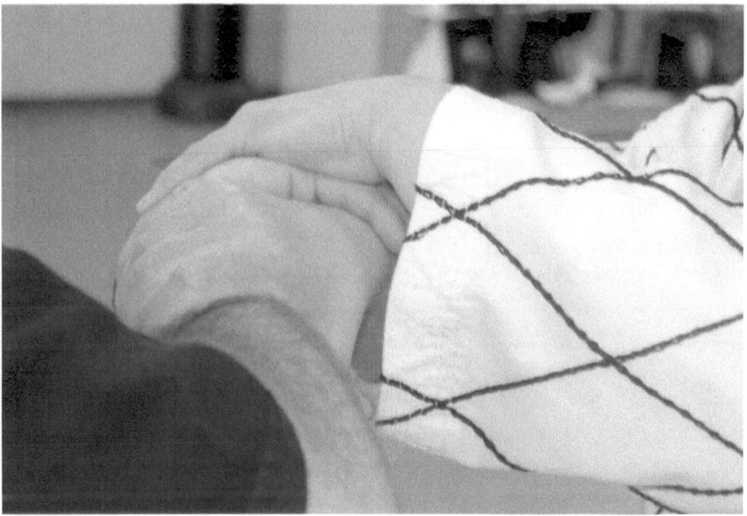

Figure 80: Finish with pressure placed downward

Notes:

The key to this technique is to make all of the circles as big as possible when rotating.

When you have the hand in position with the heel of the held hand on the opponent's wrist, make sure to lock out the wrist.

Technique Name: Elbow Attack with Arm Bar

Technique Type: Arm Bar

Target: Elbow

Steps:

1. Opponent performs an inside wrist grab, grabbing the opposite wrist.
2. Grab the holding wrist with the held hand and pull the opponent towards you.
3. Left step in with your left foot to your opponent's right foot as shown in Figure 81. You will also pull the opponent toward you in the direction of the elbow.
4. Lock out the opponent's arm; place your arm over the opponent's shoulder. Opponent's arm will be placed under your arm at the upper arm. Attempt to touch your hand to your other arm.
5. Lift up to apply pressure as shown in Figure 82.
6. Step out and to the left to twist opponent's shoulder.

Figure 81: Step to outside and apply elbow strike to opponent

Figure 82: Finish with pressure upward on elbow

Technique Name: Arm Lock

Technique Type: Joint Manipulation

Target: Wrist/Elbow

Steps:

1. Opponent performs an inside wrist grab, grabbing both wrists with each hand.
2. Left hand circles outside the opponent's right wrist as shown in Figure 83. Grab with the thumb on top with opponent's right pinky facing up.
3. Right hand grabs the opponent's right fist, holding it to the inside of the left wrist.
4. Lift the opponent's right fist while stepping forward with the right foot in Figure 84. This will apply pressure.
5. Step back and opponent will front break fall.

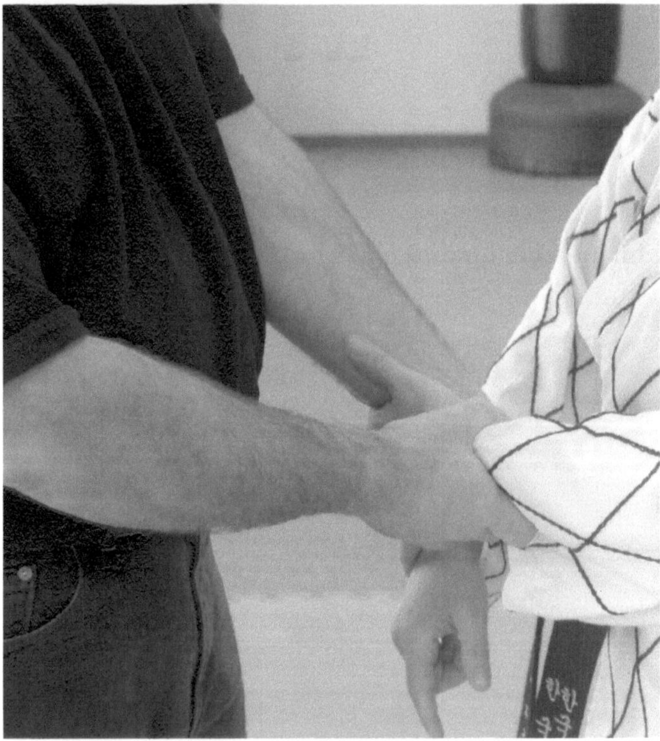

Figure 83: Left hand circles for grab

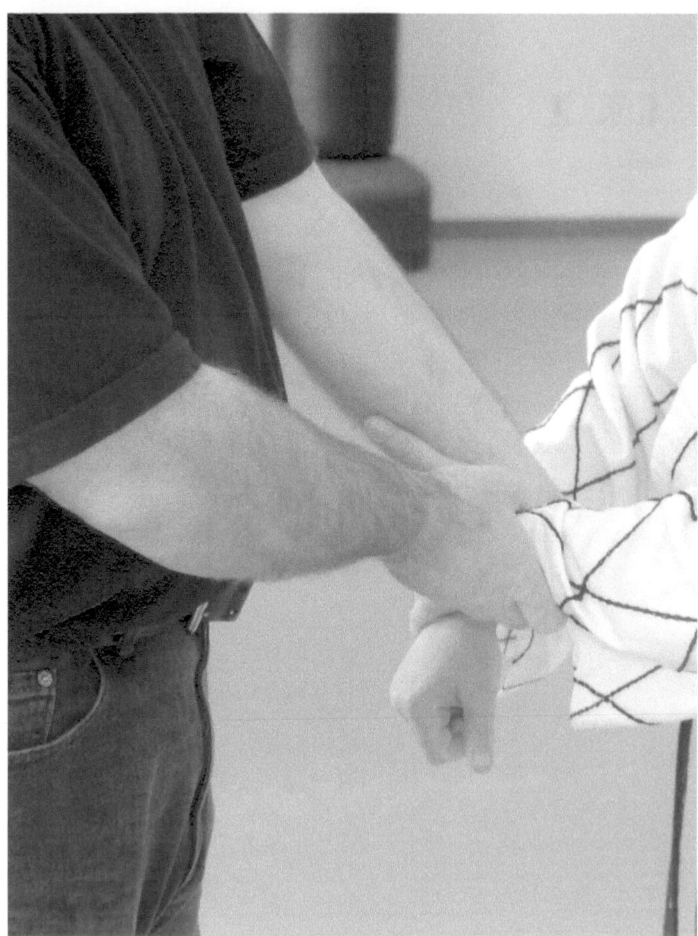

Figure 84: Lift to apply pressure

Advanced Techniques

Technique Listing

Technique Name: Inter-twined Chicken Wing

Technique Type: Joint Manipulation

Target: Shoulder

Steps:

1. Opponent grabs same side wrist. This is considered an outside wrist grab.
2. Open hand into live hand position to make room for the escape.
3. Grab with thumb on the opponent's forearm at pressure point located 2 ½ to 3 inches down from the inside of the elbow crease as shown in Figure 85. This is considered the acupressure point five of the lung meridian.
4. Step to the right and push the holding arm through as shown in Figure 86.
5. Lock the holding arm into place and move around to the back of opponent as shown in Figure 87. Make sure that the elbow is tight in to the opponent, do not go wide.
6. Bend opponent's elbow to put pressure on the holding arm.
7. Opponent kneels.

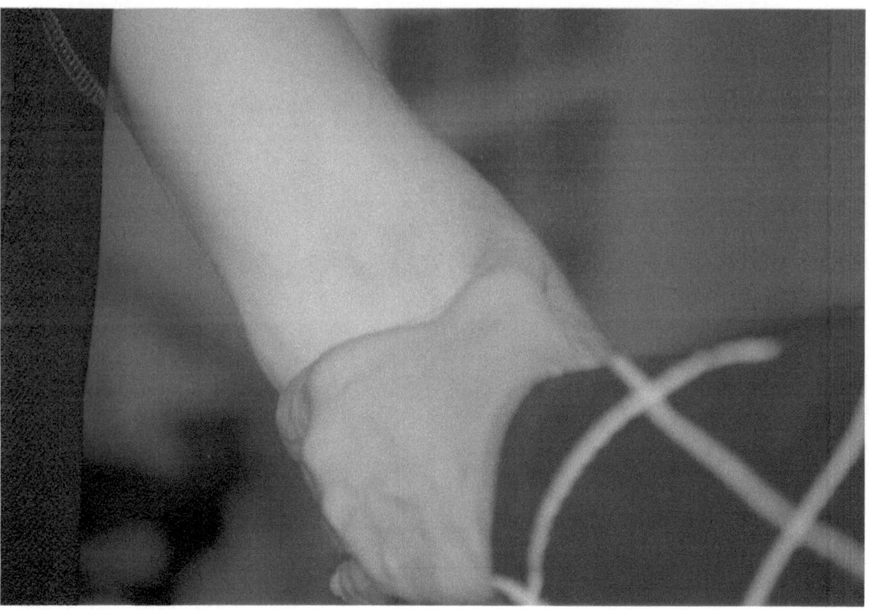

Figure 85: Grab at pressure point

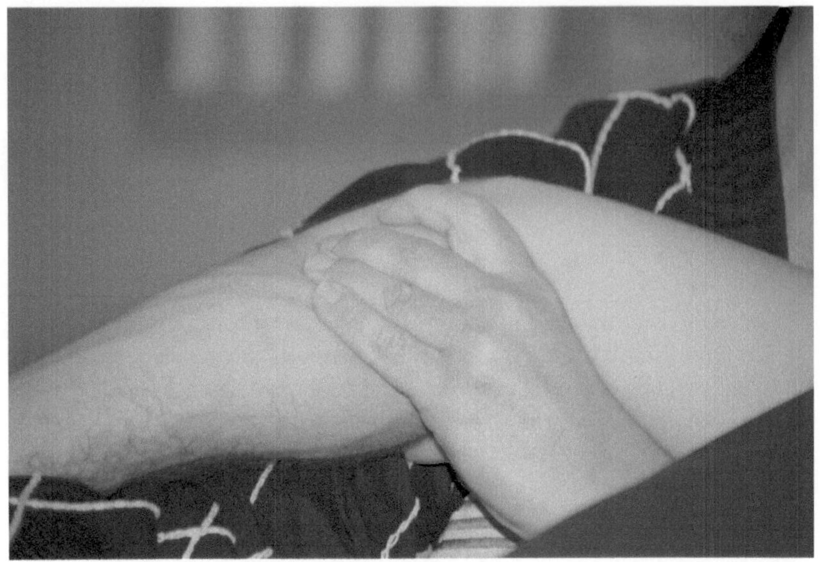

Figure 86: Step and push arm back and through

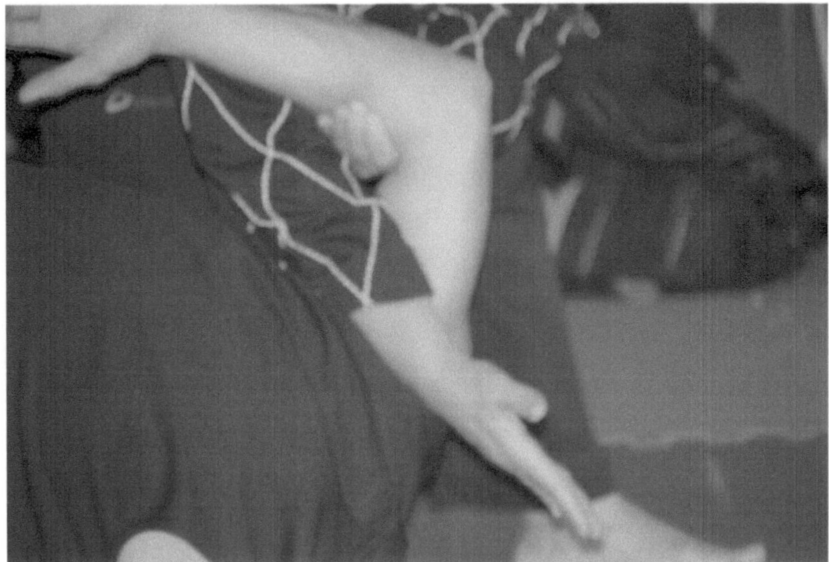

Figure 87: Finish with pressure

Notes:

This is a chicken wing variation with the arms inter-twined. The arm inter-twined within the opponent's arms can be moved like a lever to put pressure on the opponent's shoulder.

Technique Name: Wrist Lock, Arm Bar Chain with a Throw

Technique Type: Joint Manipulation and Takedown

Target: Wrist and Elbow

Steps:

1. Technique begins from a clothing grab with the opponent grabbing the top of sleeve at the wrist.
2. Grab holding hand with free hand at the opponent's wrist.
3. Open held hand into live hand position to make room for escape.
4. Rotate the held hand over the opponent's wrist in a small circle. Should be wrist bone to wrist bone. Your elbow should be at a right angle.
5. Push down on wrist and lift slightly with the left hand while stepping with the right foot. Take the right hand out. This will initiate the wrist lock as shown in Figure 88.
6. Right hand forms a knife hand and applies pressure two inches about opponent's elbow (toward the shoulder) making an arm bar situation as shown in Figure 89.
7. Re-adjust the grip on opponent's left hand. Grab at the thumb socket and turn wrist back with fingers pointing toward the opponent's shoulder as shown in Figure 90. Opponent drops to back as shown in Figure 91.

Figure 88: Initial Wrist Lock

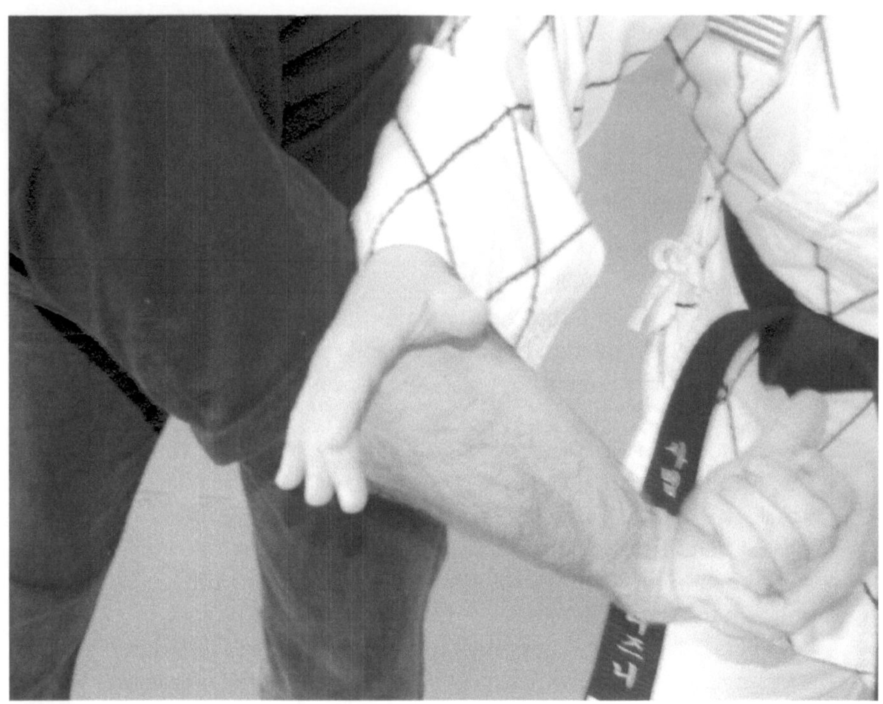

Figure 89: Transition to arm bar

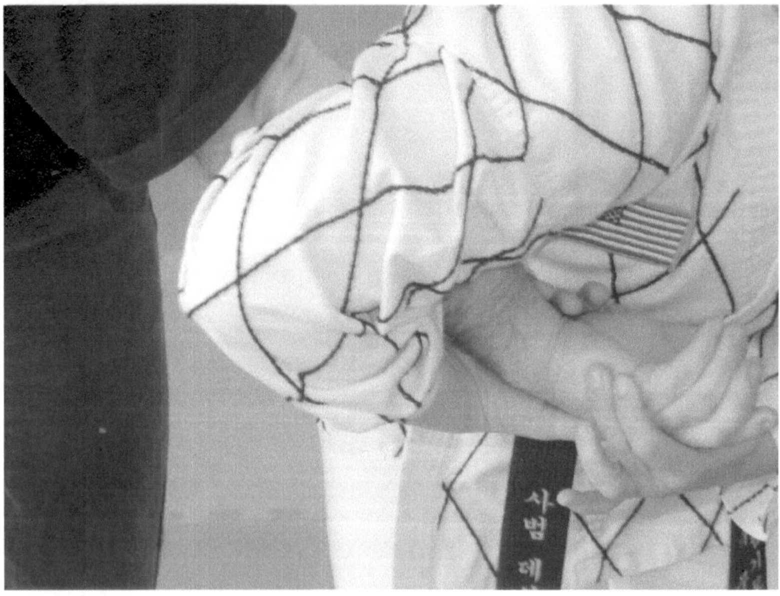

Figure 90: Readjust grip

Figure 91: Finish with throw

Notes:

Make sure to apply each technique fully before moving onto the next in the chain. You want to make sure each technique is taken to its finish before transitioning to the next one.

There are three techniques in total ending with the throw.

Technique Name: Z-lock Chain

Technique Type: Joint Manipulation

Target: Wrist

Steps:

1. Technique begins with a clothing grab with the opponent grabbing the upper arm top sleeve at the bicep as shown in Figure 92.
2. Grab the holding hand with the off hand and keep opponent's hand tight to the bicep.
3. Raise held arm up and bring elbow over the opponent's arm as shown in Figure 93. This will trap the holding hand. Place off hand between the elbow joint. Make sure the holding hand is pinky side up.
4. Release the off hand and move down to held arm at the elbow joint. Place fingers at the elbow joint and collapse arm with an inward bend at the elbow. Bring the wrist up slightly. This is the Z-lock as shown in Figure 94.
5. Lift the holding hand up to increase the pressure. Place pressure on the opponent's wrist with a twist. Pull opponent forward.
6. Opponent will front break fall.

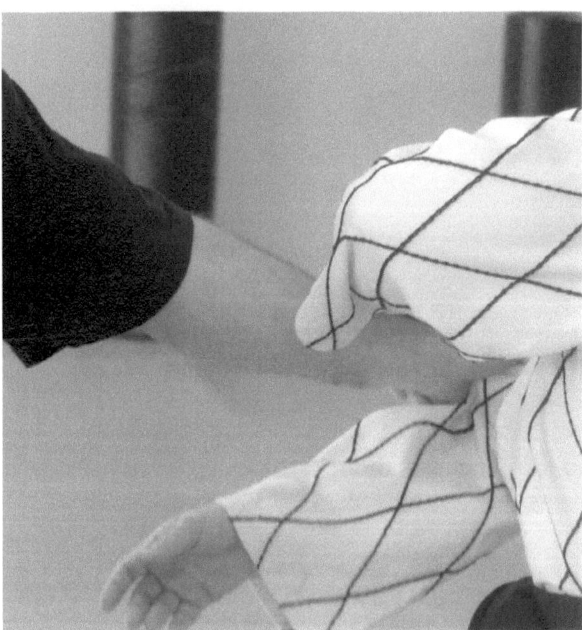

Figure 92: Initial grab

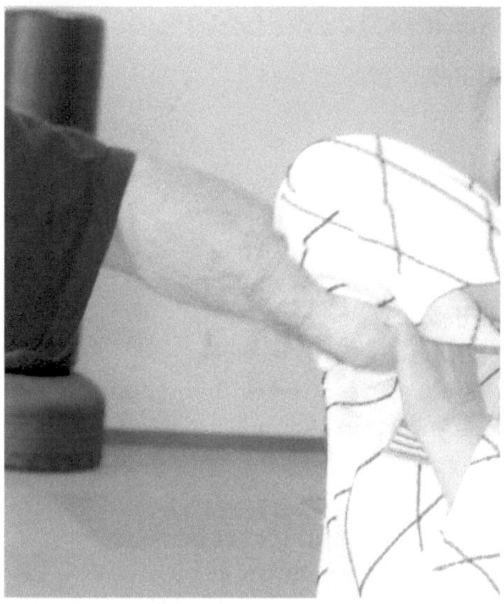

Figure 93: Elbow over to initiate lock

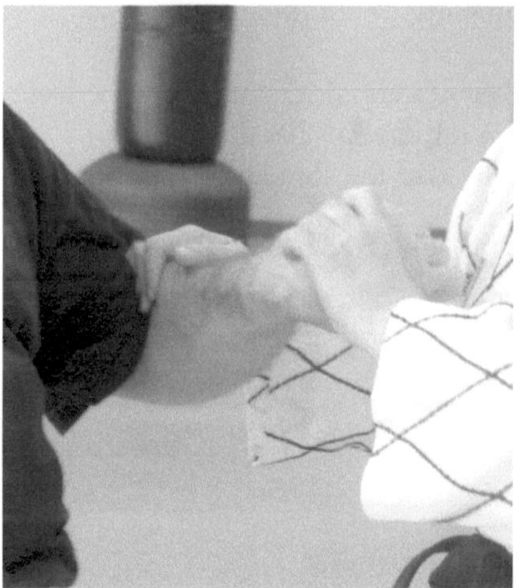

Figure 94: Z-lock to apply pressure

Notes:

Make sure the pressure is not generated by pushing down with the elbow on the forearm.

Pressure is generated by upward rotation of wrist.

Technique Name: Five Technique Chain with a Shoulder Lock Finish

Technique Type: Joint Manipulation and Projection

Target: Wrist, Elbow and Shoulder

Steps:

1. Technique begins with a clothing grab with opponent grabbing the collar at the back of the neck.
2. Left hand will hold the opponent's grip in place.
3. Right hand grabs across and secures the held hand and rotate inward into a wrist lock as shown in Figure 95.
4. Reach around with the left arm and lock the opponent's arm in a figure four arm bar.
5. Reverse the grip and grab at the thumb socket bringing opponent's arm back at the elbow as shown in Figure 96. Bring opponent down to their back. Fingers lead the body down, pointing to the ground.
6. Put the left foot under the opponent's shoulder with feet in a deep back stance. Apply pressure to opponent's elbow as shown in Figure 97.
7. Place right foot under opponent's shoulder with feet in a deep back stance. Change grip on opponent's hand and place opponent's arm on your shin. Use the shin and leg to force the opponent to their stomach.
8. Reverse the wrist lock and aim fingers toward your opponent's head. Move opponent's arm up and toward the head. This will put pressure on the shoulder.

Figure 95: Initial wrist lock with transition to arm bar

Figure 96: Reversing grip to bring opponent to their back

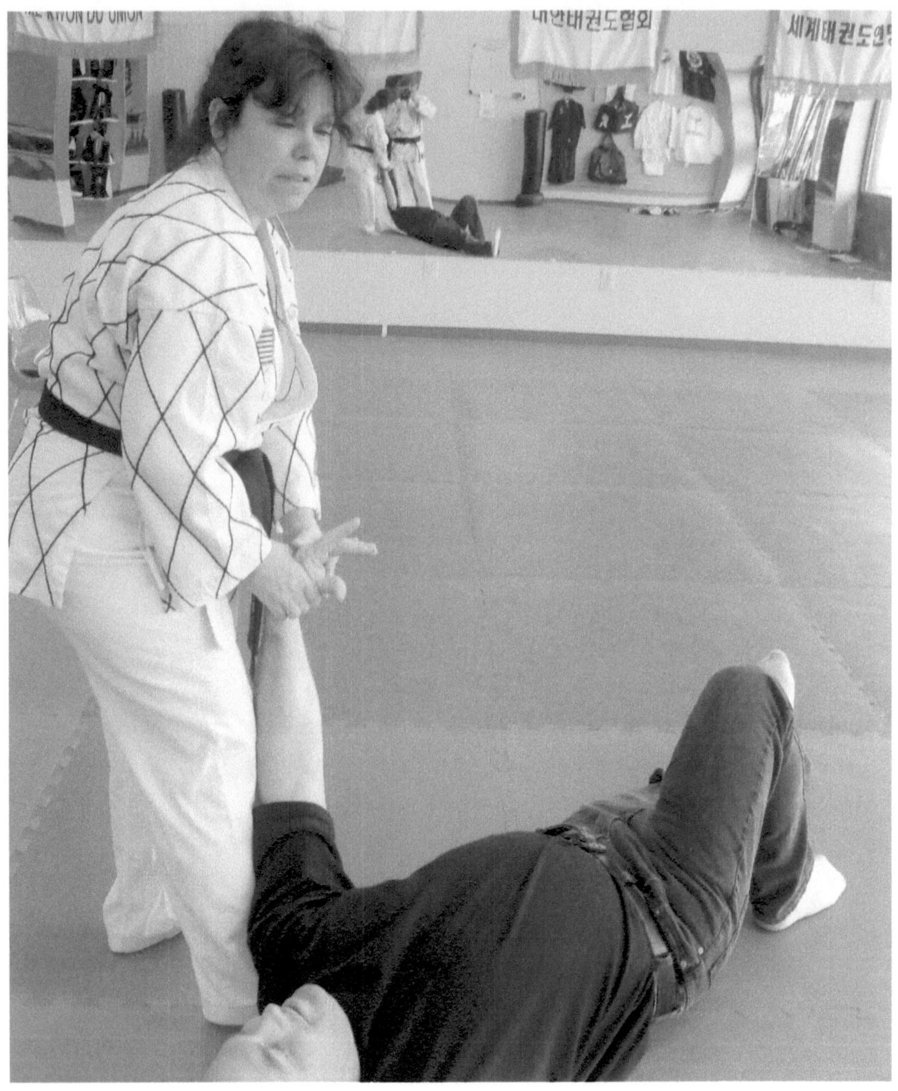

Figure 97: Takedown with initial break

Technique Name: Gooseneck Wrist Manipulation with Takedown

Technique Type: Joint Manipulation

Target: Wrist

Steps:

1. Opponent from behind grabs both shoulders with same side hands.
2. Step back and right ducking the shoulder while stepping. Circle back and under the arm.
3. Grab opponent's hand that is grasping the high shoulder with a thumb to the back of the hand as shown in Figure 98.
4. Shrug the grasped shoulder and pull the hand off. Pop the shoulder forward and step forward.
5. Grab with the thumbs to the palm of the hand, fingers to the back. Force the wrist back as shown in Figure 99.
6. Opponent bends down if done lightly; side break fall if done moderately; somersault break fall if done fully.

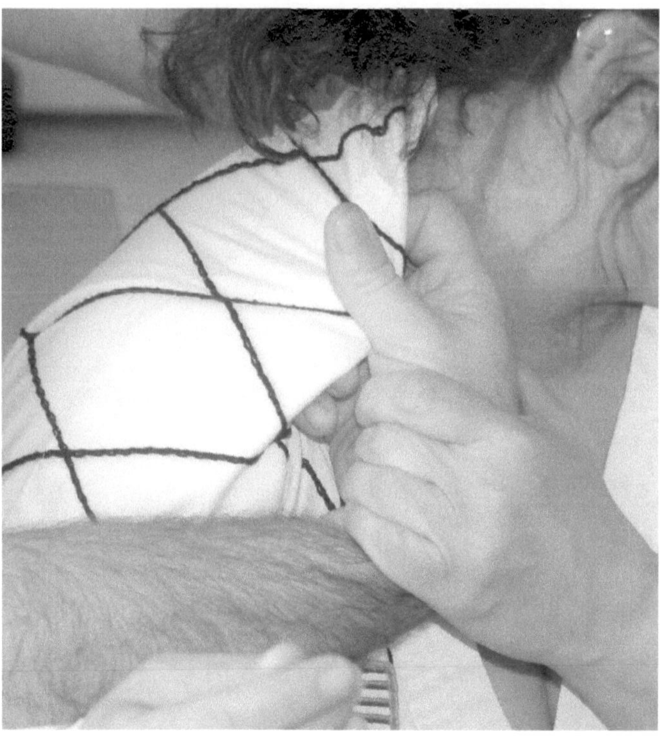

Figure 98: Shoulder shrug with wrist grab

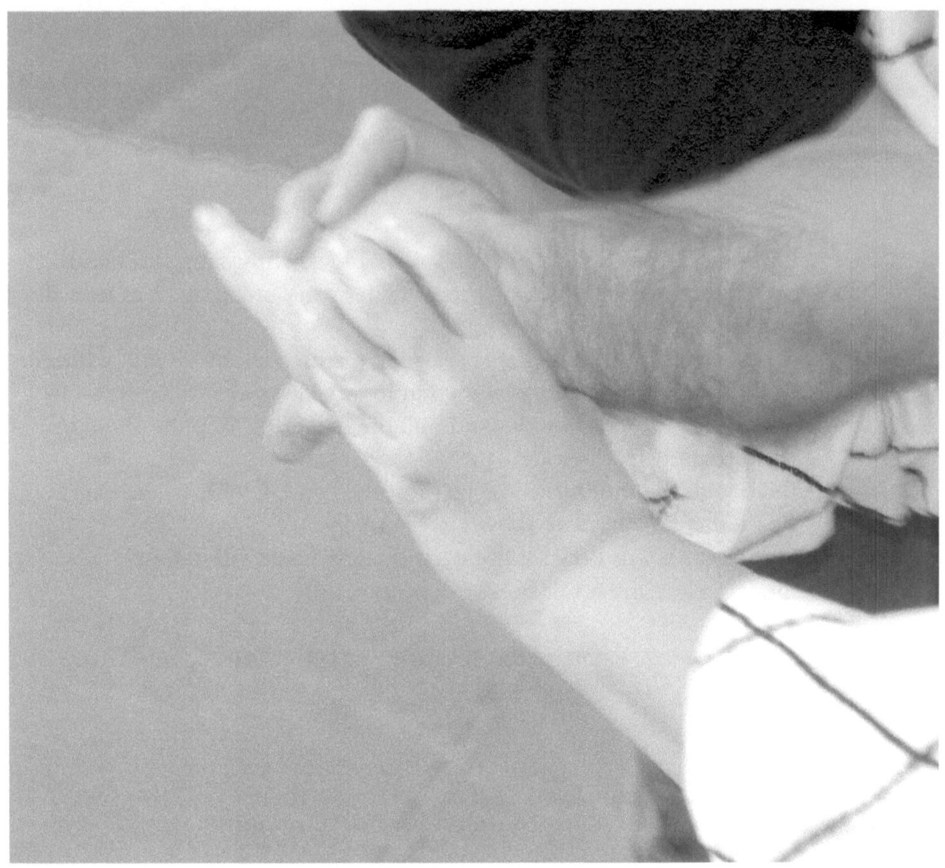

Figure 99: Gooseneck grab finish

Technique Name: Dual Arm Trapping Arm Bar

Technique Type: Arm Bar

Target: Elbow

Steps:

1. Opponent grabs from behind at the elbows with same side hands.
2. Put arms out to the side with a wide swing into a horse stance as shown in Figure 100.
3. Step behind to the right and rotate under the opponent's arm as shown in Figure 101.
4. Lock up arm at the wrist with one arm at the crook of your elbow and apply a knife hand to the opponent's elbow joint as shown in Figure 102.
5. Step in toward the opponent and apply force to the arm bar as shown in Figure 103.
6. Rotate the arm over with pressure.
7. If applied parallel to the ground, the opponent will step and tap to indicate effectiveness. If the arm bar is angled, the opponent kneels and taps.

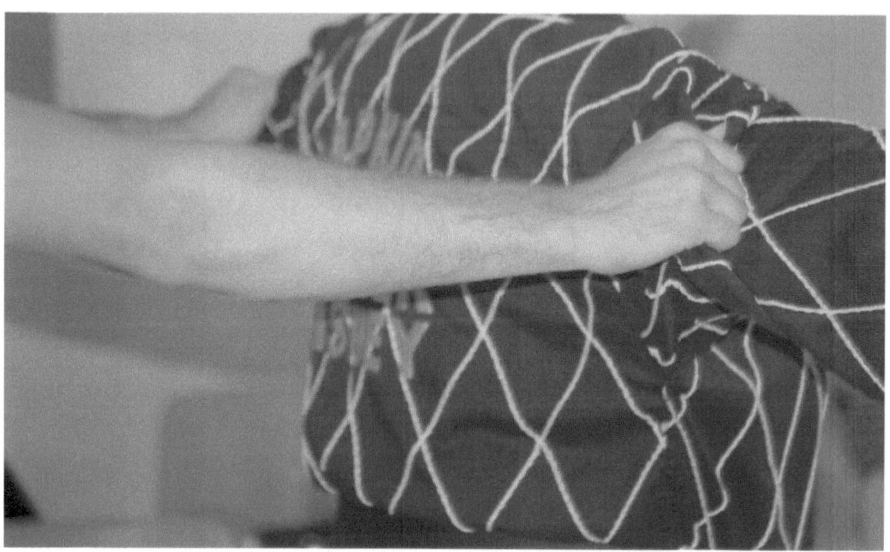

Figure 100: Start for technique with clothing grab from behind

Figure 101: Arms go wide and rotate back

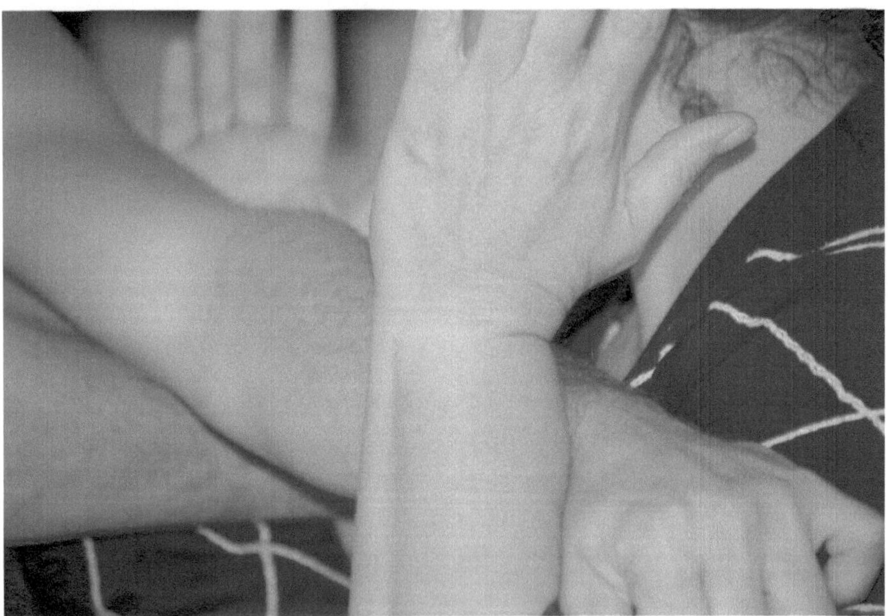

Figure 102: Initial arm trap

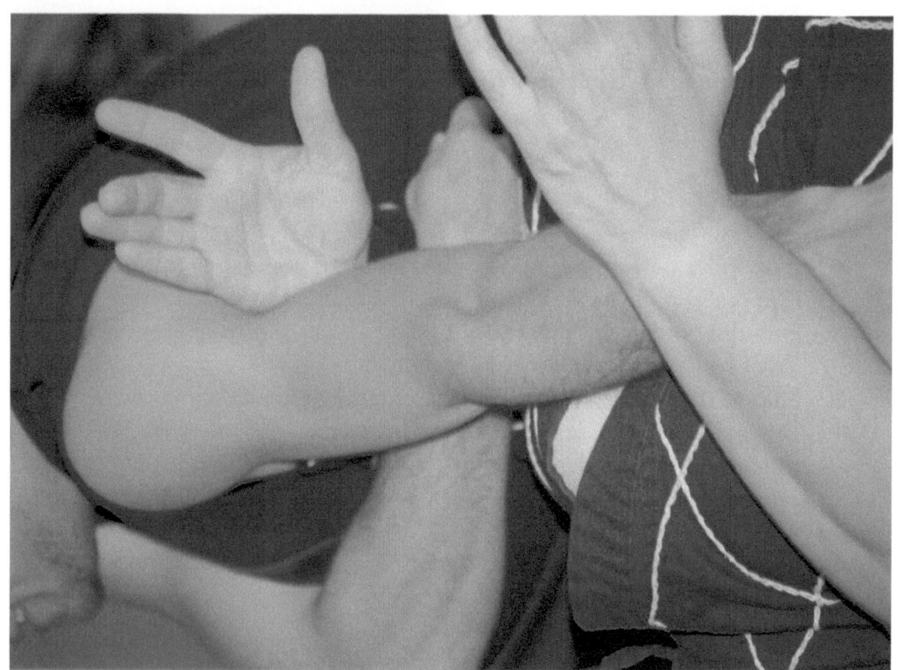

Figure 103: Finish with arm bar

Technique Name: Clamshell Wrist Lock

Technique Type: Joint Manipulation

Target: Wrist

Steps:

1. Opponent performs an inside wrist grab, grabbing the opposite wrist.
2. Opponent pulls the held hand towards them. Go with the pull and grab the holding hand with your held hand as shown in Figure 104. Pivot so that your opponent's hand is now on your back.
3. Step to the side of your opponent, parallel to the direction of the pull.
4. Bring the held arm up along your back to lock out the wrist. You will the opponent in a clamshell wrist lock as show in Figure 105.
5. Step left foot slightly behind while applying pressure to the opponent's wrist.
6. Opponent will side break fall under moderate pressure. Opponent will somersault break fall under full pressure.

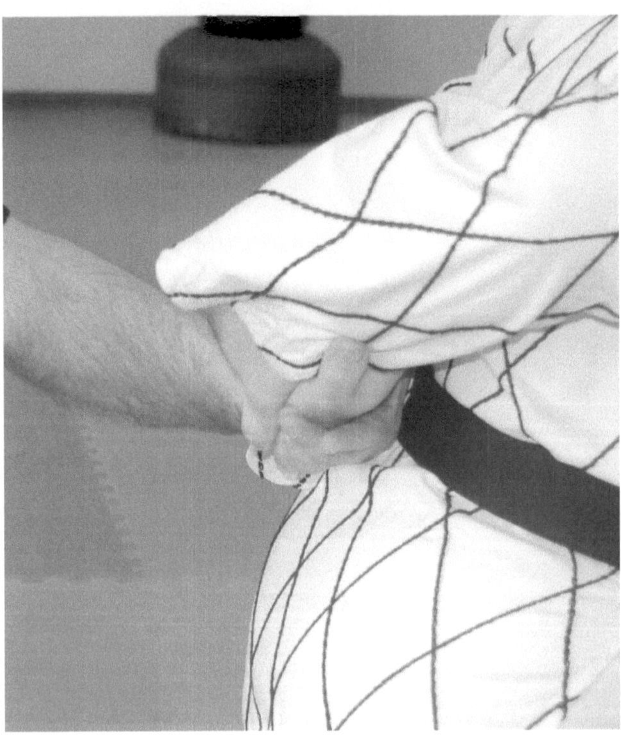

Figure 104: Initial grab

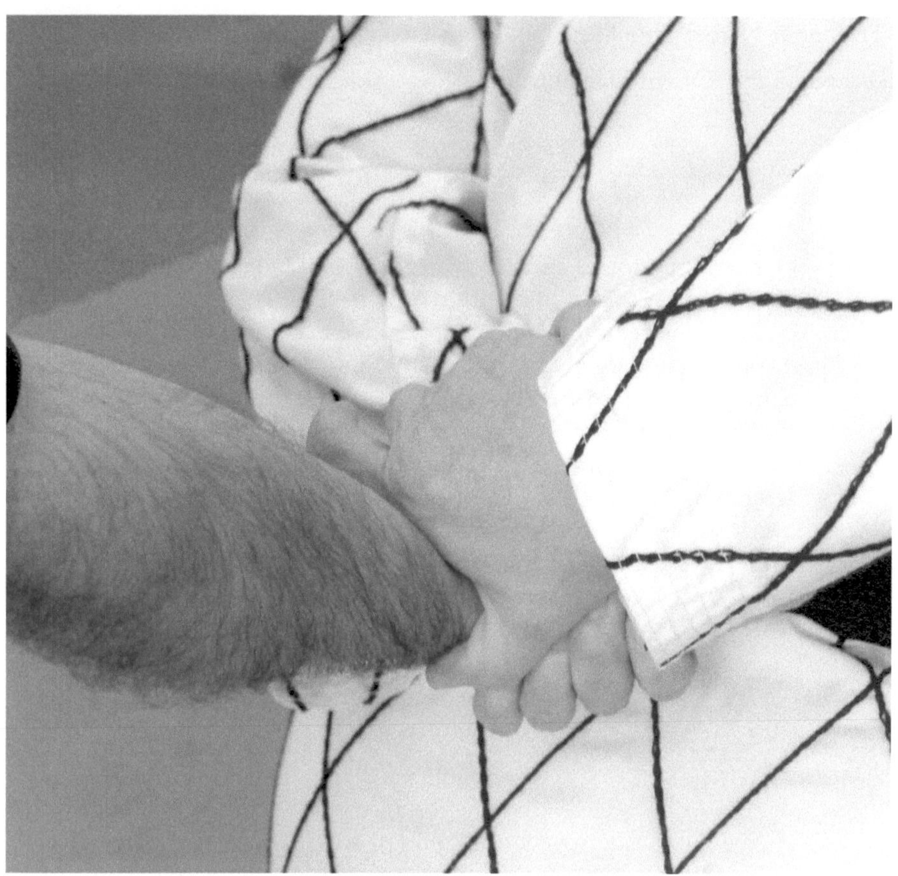

Figure 105: Close up of clamshell grab. Hands will be on top and bottom of affected hand which allows pressure to be placed on the trapped wrist.

Technique Name: Shoulder Lock From Two Handed Grab

Technique Type: Joint Manipulation

Target: Shoulder

Steps:

1. Opponent performs an inside wrist grab, grabbing the right wrist with both hands as shown in Figure 106.
2. Grab the inside of the opponent's right wrist with the held hand.
3. Apply pressure to the pressure point on the inside of the opponent's right forearm, near the elbow with the thumb of the free hand as shown in Figure 107.
4. Turn to the right so you are facing the same direction as your opponent as shown in Figure 108. At the same time, bring the opponent's arms over your head and rest them on your right shoulder.
5. Apply pressure downward onto the shoulder joint by dropping down to a knee as shown in Figure 109.

Figure 106: Initial grab for technique

Figure 107: Pressure point grab with off hand

Figure 108: Step to the right and bring arm around

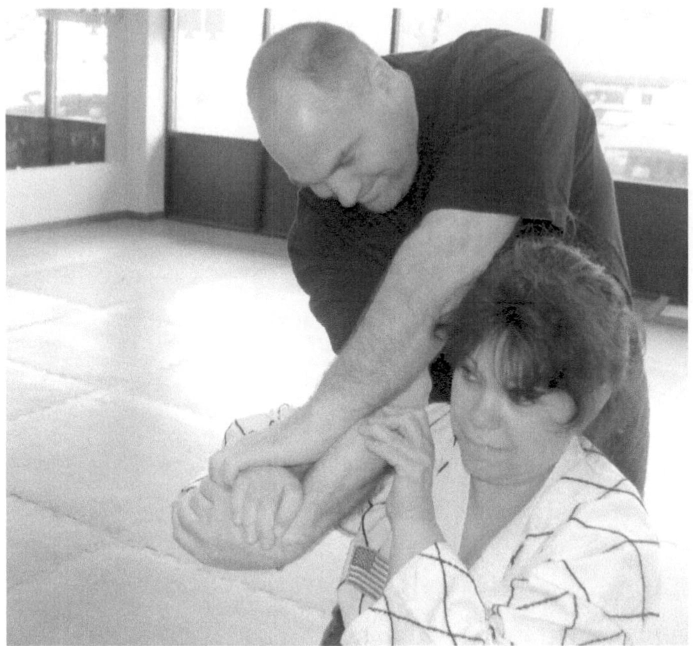

Figure 109: Finish with arm locked

Notes:

When the opponent's arm is resting on your right shoulder, the opponent's arm should be bent and the spot right above the elbow should be resting on your shoulder.

The quicker the downward drop, the more pressure on the shoulder.

Technique Name: Trapping Wrist Lock to Elbow Lock

Technique Type: Joint Manipulation

Target: Wrist/Elbow

Steps:

1. Opponent performs an inside wrist grab, grabbing both wrists with both hands.
2. Take a left adjustment step while the left hand grabs the opponent's left wrist.
3. Bend knees to lower body. Right wrist will then roll under the opponent's left hand, breaking the grip on the right hand as shown in Figure 110.
4. Left foot steps back and then straightens the right arm as shown in Figure 111.
5. Take the opponent's left hand and manipulate the arm position so that the your right forearm is two finger widths above the opponent's left elbow, toward the shoulder. This will lock out the arm as shown in Figure 112.
6. Opponent will tap to indicate effectiveness.

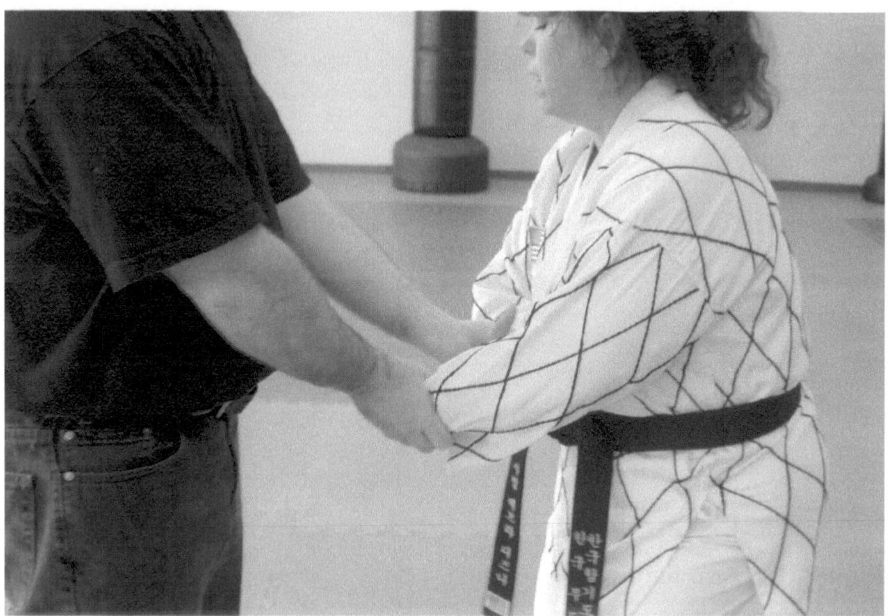

Figure 110: Right wrist rolls under the left hand to break grip

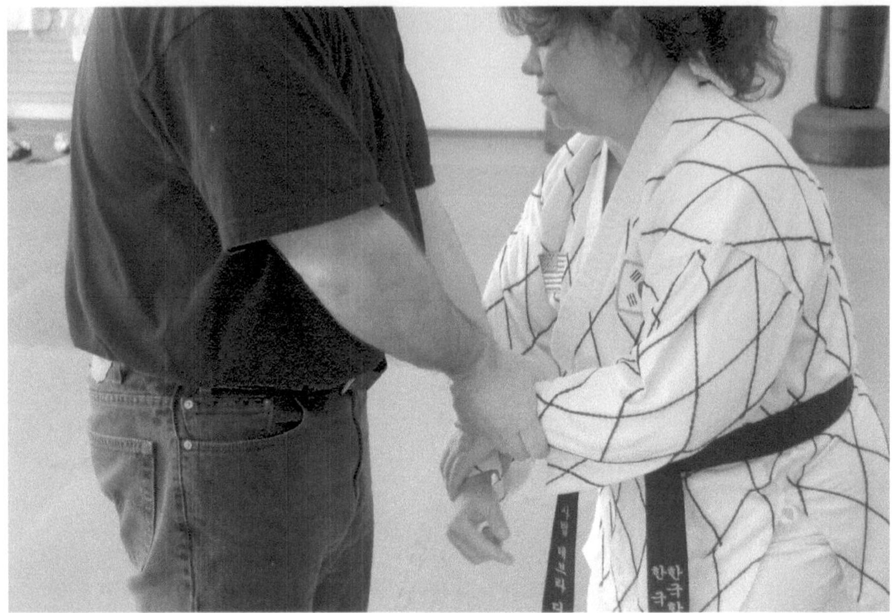

Figure 111: Grip is broken, wrist is locked

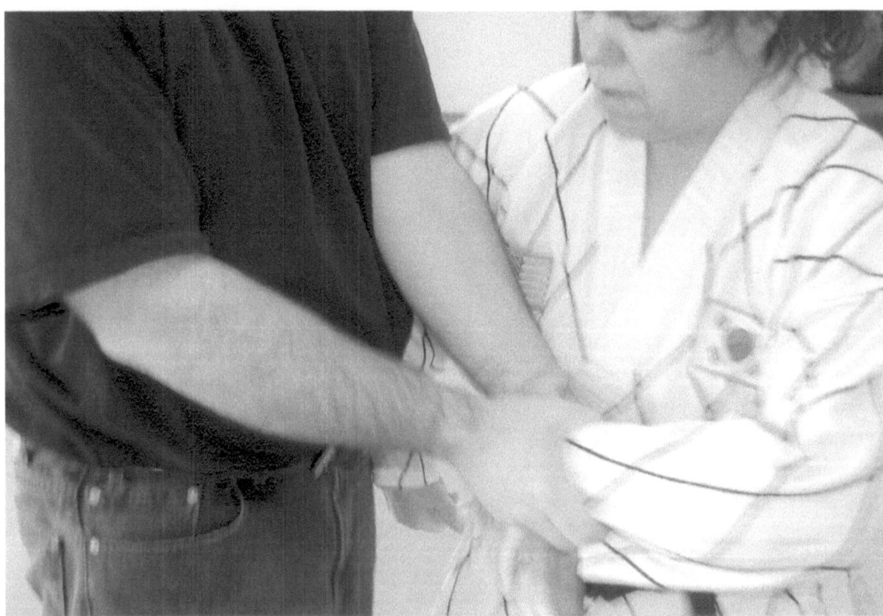

Figure 112: Arm bar finish

Technique Summary

Technique Listing

Joint Manipulations

Target: Wrist

Target: Shoulder

Target: Elbow

Targets: Wrist and Elbow

Targets: Wrist, Elbow and Shoulder

Arm Bars

About the Author

Frank Fedele

Began his training in martial arts in 1999 taking up Taekwondo and Hapkido at a school in Frederick, MD. Through hard work and a love for the art, he earned his black belt in both disciplines, reaching 2nd degree in November of 2003.

We then felt the need to explore something different, something with a little harder edge. He then branched off and trained a more hard style martial arts for a couple of years, but ultimately came back to Hapkido. He found Korean Martial Arts in Frederick, MD as a place to train and come back to his love of Hapkido.

He was eventually promoted to 4th degree in Hapkido in March of 2009 under the Korean Hapkido Federation and Grand Master Hee Wk Kim.

He wrote the Tool Box Hapkido book later in 2009 and came up with the seminar program soon after. He has been teaching at a variety of locations since receiving his 1st degree in 2002.

For more information, go to the website http://www.toolboxhapkido.com .

www.ingramcontent.com/pod-product-compliance
Ingram Content Group UK Ltd.
Pitfield, Milton Keynes, MK11 3LW, UK
UKHW041937190726
13854UKWH00004B/1636

9 780615 440576